W9-AQT-020

THE
COAST SALISH
PEOPLES

THE
COAST SALISH
PEOPLES

Frank W. Porter III

*Director, Chelsea House Foundation
for American Indian Studies*

CHELSEA HOUSE PUBLISHERS
New York   Philadelphia

On the cover A Cowichan Indian's dance rattle, made of wood painted and carved to represent a human face.

Chelsea House Publishers
Editor-in-Chief Nancy Toff
Executive Editor Remmel T. Nunn
Managing Editor Karyn Gullen Browne
Copy Chief Juliann Barbato
Picture Editor Adrian G. Allen
Art Director Maria Epes
Manufacturing Manager Gerald Levine

Indians of North America
Senior Editor Liz Sonneborn

Staff for **THE COAST SALISH**
Associate Editor Randall de Sève
Deputy Copy Chief Nicole Bowen
Copy Editor Philip Koslow
Editorial Assistant Claire Wilson
Assistant Art Director Loraine Machlin
Designer Donna Sinisgalli
Designer Assistant James Baker
Picture Researchers Susan Rupert and Joan Beard
Production Coordinator Joseph Romano

First Printing

1 3 5 7 9 8 6 4 2

Library of Congress Cataloging-in-Publication Data

Porter, Frank W., 1947–
The Coast Salish peoples / Frank W. Porter III.
    p.   cm.—(Indians of North America)
Bibliography: p.
Includes index.
Summary: Examines the culture, history, and changing fortunes of the Coast Salish Indians.
ISBN 1-55546-701-6.
    0-7910-0377-9 (pbk.)
1. Coast Salish Indians.   [1. Coast Salish Indians. 2. Indians of North America.] I. Title. II. Series: Indians of North America (Chelsea House Publishers).   89-9730
E99.S21P67   1989   CIP
970.004'979—dc20   AC

CONTENTS

INDIANS OF NORTH AMERICA

CHELSEA HOUSE PUBLISHERS

INDIANS OF NORTH AMERICA: CONFLICT AND SURVIVAL

Frank W. Porter III

> *The Indians survived our open intention of wiping them out, and since the tide turned they have even weathered our good intentions toward them, which can be much more deadly.*
>
> John Steinbeck
> *America and Americans*

When Europeans first reached the North American continent, they found hundreds of tribes occupying a vast and rich country. The newcomers quickly recognized the wealth of natural resources. They were not, however, so quick or willing to recognize the spiritual, cultural, and intellectual riches of the people they called Indians.

The Indians of North America examines the problems that develop when people with different cultures come together. For American Indians, the consequences of their interaction with non-Indian people have been both productive and tragic. The Europeans believed they had "discovered" a "New World," but their religious bigotry, cultural bias, and materialistic world view kept them from appreciating and understanding the people who lived in it. All too often they attempted to change the way of life of the indigenous people. The Spanish conquistadores wanted the Indians as a source of labor. The Christian missionaries, many of whom were English, viewed them as potential converts. French traders and trappers used the Indians as a means to obtain pelts. As Francis Parkman, the 19th-century historian, stated, "Spanish civilization crushed the Indian; English civilization scorned and neglected him; French civilization embraced and cherished him."

Nearly 500 years later, many people think of American Indians as curious vestiges of a distant past, waging a futile war to survive in a Space Age society. Even today, our understanding of the history and culture of American Indians is too often derived from unsympathetic, culturally biased, and inaccurate reports. The American Indian, described and portrayed in thousands of movies, television programs, books, articles, and government studies, has either been raised to the status of the "noble savage" or disparaged as the "wild Indian" who resisted the westward expansion of the American frontier.

Where in this popular view are the real Indians, the human beings and communities whose ancestors can be traced back to ice-age hunters? Where are the creative and indomitable people whose sophisticated technologies used the natural resources to ensure their survival, whose military skill might even have prevented European settlement of North America if not for devastating epidemics and disruption of the ecology? Where are the men and women who are today diligently struggling to assert their legal rights and express once again the value of their heritage?

The various Indian tribes of North America, like people everywhere, have a history that includes population expansion, adaptation to a range of regional environments, trade across wide networks, internal strife, and warfare. This was the reality. Europeans justified their conquests, however, by creating a mythical image of the New World and its native people. In this myth, the New World was a virgin land, waiting for the Europeans. The arrival of Christopher Columbus ended a timeless primitiveness for the original inhabitants.

Also part of this myth was the debate over the origins of the American Indians. Fantastic and diverse answers were proposed by the early explorers, missionairies, and settlers. Some thought that the Indians were descended from the Ten Lost Tribes of Israel, others that they were descended from inhabitants of the lost continent of Atlantis. One writer suggested that the Indians had reached North America in another Noah's ark.

A later myth, perpetrated by many historians, focused on the relentless persecution during the past five centuries until only a scattering of these "primitive" people remained to be herded onto reservations. This view fails to chronicle the overt and covert ways in which the Indians successfully coped with the intruders.

All of these myths presented one-sided interpretations that ignored the complexity of European and American events and policies. All left serious questions unanswered. What were the origins of the American Indians? Where did they come from? How and when did they get to the New World? What was their life—their culture—really like?

In the late 1800s, anthropologists and archaeologists in the Smithsonian Institution's newly created Bureau of American Ethnology in Washington,

D.C., began to study scientifically the history and culture of the Indians of North America. They were motivated by an honest belief that the Indians were on the verge of extinction and that along with them would vanish their languages, religious beliefs, technology, myths, and legends. These men and women went out to visit, study, and record data from as many Indian communities as possible before this information was forever lost.

By this time there was a new myth in the national consciousness. American Indians existed as figures in the American past. They had performed a historical mission. They had challenged white settlers who trekked across the continent. Once conquered, however, they were supposed to accept graciously the way of life of their conquerors.

The reality again was different. American Indians resisted both actively and passively. They refused to lose their unique identity, to be assimilated into white society. Many whites viewed the Indians not only as members of a conquered nation but also as "inferior" and "unequal." The rights of the Indians could be expanded, contracted, or modified as the conquerors saw fit. In every generation, white society asked itself what to do with the American Indians. Their answers have resulted in the twists and turns of federal Indian policy.

There were two general approaches. One way was to raise the Indians to a "higher level" by "civilizing" them. Zealous missionaries considered it their Christian duty to elevate the Indian through conversion and scanty education. The other approach was to ignore the Indians until they disappeared under pressure from the ever-expanding white society. The myth of the "vanishing Indian" gave stronger support to the latter option, helping to justify the taking of the Indians' land.

Prior to the end of the 18th century, there was no national policy on Indians simply because the American nation has not yet come into existence. American Indians similarly did not possess a political or social unity with which to confront the various Europeans. They were not homogeneous. Rather, they were loosely formed bands and tribes, speaking nearly 300 languages and thousands of dialects. The collective identity felt by Indians today is a result of their common experiences of defeat and/or mistreatment at the hands of whites.

During the colonial period, the British crown did not have a coordinated policy toward the Indians of North America. Specific tribes (most notably the Iroquois and the Cherokee) became military and political pawns used by both the crown and the individual colonies. The success of the American Revolution brought no immediate change. When the United States acquired new territory from France and Mexico in the early 19th century, the federal government wanted to open this land to settlement by homesteaders. But the Indian tribes that lived on this land had signed treaties with European governments assuring their title to the land. Now the United States assumed legal responsibility for honoring these treaties.

At first, President Thomas Jefferson believed that the Louisiana Purchase contained sufficient land for both the Indians and the white population. Within a generation, though, it became clear that the Indians would not be allowed to remain. In the 1830s the federal government began to coerce the eastern tribes to sign treaties agreeing to relinquish their ancestral land and move west of the Mississippi River. Whenever these negotiations failed, President Andrew Jackson used the military to remove the Indians. The southeastern tribes, promised food and transportation during their removal to the West, were instead forced to walk the "Trail of Tears." More than 4,000 men, woman, and children died during this forced march. The "removal policy" was successful in opening the land to homesteaders, but it created enormous hardships for the Indians.

By 1871 most of the tribes in the United States had signed treaties ceding most or all of their ancestral land in exchange for reservations and welfare. The treaty terms were intended to bind both parties for all time. But in the General Allotment Act of 1887, the federal government changed its policy again. Now the goal was to make tribal members into individual landowners and farmers, encouraging their absorption into white society. This policy was advantageous to whites who were eager to acquire Indian land, but it proved disastrous for the Indians. One hundred thirty-eight million acres of reservation land were subdivided into tracts of 160, 80, or as little as 40 acres, and allotted tribe members on an individual basis. Land owned in this way was said to have "trust status" and could not be sold. But the surplus land—all Indian land not allotted to individuals—was opened (for sale) to white settlers. Ultimately, more than 90 million acres of land were taken from the Indians by legal and illegal means.

The resulting loss of land was a catastrophe for the Indians. It was necessary to make it illegal for Indians to sell their land to non-Indians. The Indian Reorganization Act of 1934 officially ended the allotment period. Tribes that voted to accept the provisions of this act were reorganized, and an effort was made to purchase land within preexisting reservations to restore an adequate land base.

Ten years later, in 1944, federal Indian policy again shifted. Now the federal government wanted to get out of the "Indian business." In 1953 an act of Congress named specific tribes whose trust status was to be ended "at the earliest possible time." This new law enabled the United States to end unilaterally, whether the Indians wished it or not, the special status that protected the land in Indian tribal reservations. In the 1950s federal Indian policy was to transfer federal responsibility and jurisdiction to state governments, encourage the physical relocation of Indian peoples from reservations to urban areas, and hasten the termination, or extinction, of tribes.

Between 1954 and 1962 Congress passed specific laws authorizing the termination of more than 100 tribal groups. The stated purpose of the termination policy was to ensure the full and complete integration of Indians into American society. However, there is a less benign way to interpret this legislation. Even as termination was being discussed in Congress, 133 separate bills were introduced to permit the transfer of trust land ownership from Indians to non-Indians.

With the Johnson administration in the 1960s the federal government began to reject termination. In the 1970s yet another Indian policy emerged. Known as "self-determination," it favored keeping the protective role of the federal government while increasing tribal participation in, and control of, important areas of local government. In 1983 President Reagan, in a policy statement on Indian affairs, restated the unique "government is government" relationship of the United States with the Indians. However, federal programs since then have moved toward transferring Indian affairs to individual states, which have long desired to gain control of Indian land and resources.

As long as American Indians retain power, land, and resources that are coveted by the states and the federal government, there will continue to be a "clash of cultures," and the issues will be contested in the courts, Congress, the White House, and even in the international human rights community. To give all Americans a greater comprehension of the issues and conflicts involving American Indians today is a major goal of this series. These issues are not easily understood, nor can these conflicts be readily resolved. The study of North American Indian history and culture is a necessary and important step toward that comprehension. All Americans must learn the history of the relations between the Indians and the federal government, recognize the unique legal status of the Indians, and understand the heritage and cultures of the Indians of North America.

Chief Seattle, pictured here in 1865, represented the Duwamish and Suquamish Indians during their treaty negotiations with Washington Territory governor Isaac Ingalls Stevens in the 1850s.

IN THE MIDST
OF PLENTY

Yonder sky that has wept tears of compassion upon my people for centuries untold, and which to us appears changeless and eternal, may change. Today is fair. Tomorrow it may be overcast with clouds. . . . Big Chief [President Millard Fillmore] at Washington sends us greetings of friendship and good will. This is kind of him for we know he has little need of our friendship in return. His people are many. They are like the grass that covers vast prairies. My people are few. They resemble the scattering trees of a storm-swept plain. The Great—and I presume—good White Chief sends us word that he wishes to buy our lands but is willing to allow us enough to live comfortably. This indeed appears just, even generous, for the Red Man no longer has rights that he need respect.

It matters little where we pass the remnant of our days. They will not be many.

Chief Seattle, a leader of the Duwamish and Suquamish Indians, made this eloquent speech in 1855. The occasion was the negotiation of the Treaty of Point Elliott, in which his people ceded most of their lands to the U.S. government. Even as he was signing this document, the chief astutely recognized that the treaty's provisions would ultimately lead to tragedy for him and his followers.

Two years earlier, in 1853, what is now the state of Washington had become a territory of the United States. Although many Indians lived on this land, they were not consulted about this change in the status of their ancestral home. Only months later, when Congress authorized funds to survey several routes for a proposed transcontinental railroad, did representatives of the federal government begin to deal officially with the native population.

Isaac Ingalls Stevens, who had been appointed both governor and superintendent of Indian affairs in the new territory, was given the responsibility of surveying the northernmost possible railway routes. Before he could do this, however, he had to find a solution to the question of Indian land rights in Washington Territory. Because of a lack of treaties and the illegal taking of Indian lands by newly arrived non-Indian settlers, hostilities between Indians and whites were already widespread. In this tense situation, Governor Stevens immediately set out to extinguish Indian land ownership in Washington Territory.

Within a few months, Stevens had persuaded the leaders of approximately 6,000 Indians in the Puget Sound area to sign treaties at Point Elliott, Point No Point, Neah Bay, Medicine Creek, and Quinault River. In the treaties, these Indians gave up claims to most of their land. In return, the government was to provide them with specific goods and services and with reservation land that was to be occupied and used by Indians only. The governor soon negotiated similar treaties with other Washington Territory Indians. Within a year, the representatives of approximately 17,000 Indians had ceded more than 64 million acres in the Northwest.

Although Governor Stevens believed that the terms of his treaties were fair and just, Indians throughout the Puget Sound area soon began to have second thoughts. But it was too late. Even before Congress ratified the trea-

ties, settlers thronged into the territory, clearing land and building homesteads. Specific clauses in the treaties prohibited the Indians from defending themselves and their land. Those who did resist were diligently hunted down and punished by regular army troops and local militia. Stevens's single-minded effort to extinguish the Indians' claim to their land had been achieved, but at a tremendous cost to the Indians of Puget Sound and the entire Northwest.

Before their first contact with white people, the Indians in what became Washington Territory had lived in much the same way for thousands of years. Among the groups in the area were the Coast Salish peoples, who lived west of the Cascade Mountains between central Oregon and the southern portion of what is today British Columbia, Canada. When European explorers first encountered the Coast Salish in 1774, these Indians numbered several thousand and lived in villages scattered on the coast and islands of the Puget Sound and in the river valleys of the area. Behind these villages stood dark, foreboding, and impenetrable forests and the slopes of the high Cascade and Rocky mountain ranges. In front of the villages stretched the open sea. Although somewhat geographically isolated from each other, villagers constructed highly efficient sea and river canoes that enabled them to maintain contact with their neighbors. For this reason, Indians from the Coast Salish villages had similar ways of life. They also spoke dialects of the Coast

A Clallam father giving his sons lessons in fishing and navigation on the Strait of Juan de Fuca at the end of the 19th century.

Salish language. The name of each village was derived from the name of the Salishan dialect spoken by its residents. Dialects varied slightly between neighboring villages but became increasingly distinct as distance between the villages increased.

The most important political and landholding unit among the Coast Salish was the village. Villages usually

WHY THE PUGET SOUND INDIANS SPEAK SO MANY LANGUAGES

The Coast Salish peoples created myths to explain the natural world around them. These stories, which were passed from one generation to the next by tribal elders, varied from village to village. Certain themes, however, such as the origins of sacred animals and forces of nature, remained constant.

The following is an excerpt from a Snohomish origin myth, told by Chief William Shelton, from Indian Legends of the Pacific Northwest, *by Ella E. Clark.*

"In the beginning, the Creator and Changer made the world. He created first in the East. Then he slowly came westward, creating as he came. With him he brought many languages. He gave a different language to each group of people he created.

"When he reached Puget Sound, he liked it so well that he decided that he would go no farther. But he had many languages left. These he scattered all around Puget Sound and to the north, along the waters there. That is why there are so many different languages spoken by the Indians in the Puget Sound country."

consisted of three to five large plank houses and several smaller ones. All of the houses were built for multifamily use. There is archaeological evidence of single houses being as long as 1,000 feet, big enough to house an entire village. Villages ranged in size from 20 to—on rare occasions—1,000 people. Because of the early disruption of Coast Salish culture by Europeans, there are few records of traditional Coast Salish family structure. However, the prevailing group was an extended family, composed of individuals descended from the same ancestors.

Families occupied the villages during the winter months, between November and March. During the spring and summer, family members left the villages and moved to temporary camps near the mountains, on the riverbanks, and along the Puget Sound to collect the winter supply of food. From their distinct locations, family members performed various food-gathering tasks, including hunting, gathering, and fishing. Once the food was collected, it was prepared and brought back to the permanent winter village for storage.

Salmon was the Indians' staple food. Using spears and dip nets, the Coast Salish caught king, silver, humpback, and dog salmon as well as steelhead trout, halibut, and cod. The Coast Salish also placed fencelike wooden enclosures, called weirs, in narrow streams to trap these fish so that they could be caught more easily.

Salmon runs occurred in the same season every year. In late summer and early fall, great numbers of one type of salmon appeared at the mouth of a river or stream. After a short time, they began to swim upriver to their spawning grounds. The annual runs of salmon provided a year-round supply of food for the Coast Salish, who smoked or dried their surplus fish and stored it for use during the winter months. So important was salmon to these people that during the 1854–55 treaty talks, one Indian remarked that if he went three days without salmon his heart would fail him.

In addition to the catch from the rivers and seas, Coast Salish women and children gathered shellfish from the beaches and collected wild plant foods such as camas (lilies with edible bulbs), ferns, and roots. Men also hunted sea mammals and waterfowl—especially mallard ducks—and stalked beaver, bear, deer, and elk to add to the food supply.

Coast Salish peoples were highly conscious of social standing, and class structures existed within the villages. Basically, there were three classes: nobles, commoners, and slaves. The two most important factors in determining rank were material wealth and kinship.

Nobles had inherited wealth, married into wealthy families, proved their status through achievements in war, or had large families of industrious wives and children who had assisted them in gaining their status. Some of these noble families claimed ancestral roots going back to the beginning of the world. Often some of the myths supporting these claims were symbolized by the figures carved on totem poles. Totem poles, carved from cedar logs, displayed elaborate representations of animals and supernatural beings. They honored deceased chiefs and marked the graves of other important people. They also served as house posts, which generally honored a family's history.

Commoners were usually the poor relatives of a rich man. They might live in their noble relative's house and do routine domestic chores for him. A commoner could possibly move up in rank through marriage, special skills, or proven ability in battle.

Slaves, who were not related to nobles or commoners, composed a separate class. They had been captured in warfare or had been obtained in trade with other Indians. Slaves had very little hope of improving their position.

A wealthy man sometimes had several wives; quite often they were sisters. Marriages were contracted by the groom's family paying a dowry to the bride's family. Later, her relatives gave gifts of equal value to the groom's family. Each person typically married someone from another village, and the couple lived with the groom's family. Marriages between the members of different villages assured peaceful relations, trade arrangements, and alliances in the event of hostilities.

Political organization among the Coast Salish was poorly defined and fairly loose. No one political figure had power over the entire group. Consequently, the Coast Salish peoples never

Spearfishing for salmon, a staple of the Coast Salish diet, in 1909.

considered themselves a unified nation or acted as one. Instead, they viewed themselves as members of distinct villages or kin groups.

Although federal officials, anthropologists, and other social scientists often refer to a number of villages located in a particular area as a *tribe*, this term does not accurately describe the Coast Salish. At the time of contact with non-Indian people, each Coast Salish village was an autonomous political unit. Nevertheless, in order to simplify dealings with the Indians, government officials grouped these numerous self-governing villages into a smaller number of, what they called, tribes. Such new groupings and terminology would complicate Indian policy in years to come.

The fundamental social and political group within each village was the extended family. Each extended family had a series of landholdings on which it had the exclusive right to fish, hunt, and gather berries and weaving materials. Extended families also had nonmaterial possessions, such as the right to use crests representing animals or spirits that had been important to their ancestors, to perform particular ceremonies, and to bear certain names.

The chief was the custodian of these rights. He was usually the oldest member of the group and thought to be the most direct descendant of the family's lineal ancestor. Occasionally, a younger, more able relative could be chief in the event that the older leader gave up his position. The chief's younger broth-

A 1905 photograph of a house post made of cedar. The carvings probably represent the noble ancestry of an Indian chief or other leader.

ers were next in rank and were his presumed heirs.

Among the chief's responsibilities were deciding when to move from winter to summer villages, bestowing hereditary names, deciding on songs and dances to be used in ceremonies, and maintaining peaceful relations within the village. The better use the chief made of these powers, the more prestigious his village became in the eyes of the other groups.

Other individuals who were highly regarded in the village were the *shamans*. The shamans were a special group of men and women who knew how to cure illnesses. A person could become a shaman by acquiring one or more spirits who helped shamans cure their patients. These spirits could appear to men or women, but woman shamans were rare and not very powerful. The spirits they received were small because the women were not considered strong enough to receive big spirits. Bigger, powerful spirits were acquired by men who, to get them, fasted longer and endured more hardships than the women.

When young boys or girls sought shamanistic spirits, they did not attempt to practice until they had acquired six or more spirits. They were seldom recognized as shamans until they had actually practiced and achieved cures, by which time they were usually in their mid-twenties.

It could be dangerous to receive a shamanistic spirit. One story tells of a man who received two spirits at the same time. The spirits began to fight over him, and, frightened, he ran away. His body was later found twisted and eaten by worms. Because he was a coward, the spirits had turned their powers against him.

A person who became ill would, if possible, visit the shaman. Otherwise, the shaman would come to the patient's house. The shamans used several methods to cure illness. These included sucking the sickness directly out of the afflicted area of the body with a hollowed-out animal bone or cedar stick; manually pulling the sickness out of the patient; bleeding the sick person to withdraw the "bad" blood; touching and stroking the affected part of the body; and singing special songs.

Some illnesses were believed to be caused by the loss of one's soul or spirit, in which case the shaman would call on his spirit helpers to set out in search of the strayed soul. Villagers representing the spirit helpers would then dramatize a long journey across streams and over rough ground, on foot or in a so-called spirit canoe, tracing the path of the lost spirit. This healing ceremony would take place within or near the house. It would be performed in pantomime or narrated by one of the participants in a low voice.

The shaman lived in a communal house with relatives, unless he was wealthy enough to possess his own house. Although the shaman was frequently well paid for his services, he never accumulated as much wealth as a chief, who inherited the right to share

A beautiful Coast Salish spirit canoe and wood carving, probably of Duwamish origin, photographed in 1909. Spirit canoes were used to symbolically retrieve the strayed souls of the ill.

in the entire village's produce. In the event that a patient died, the shaman could be obligated to return to the deceased's family part or all of the goods he had been paid for his services.

One of the most important social functions among the Coast Salish was the *potlatch*. The potlatch was a great feast, during which gifts were distributed to the guests. There were a variety of reasons for hosting a potlatch. Most often, a potlatch was given to confirm the status of a chief. The chief might host a potlatch years after attaining his position to show he was worthy of the post. Additionally, potlatches were hosted to celebrate a marriage, inaugurate a new house, establish a youth as heir to the chief, and mark a death.

Although one individual held the place of honor at the potlatch, it was actually a village undertaking, with everyone in the extended family giving gifts. The gifts ranged from cedar bark blankets to canoes to robes made of animal pelts, depending on the rank of the person receiving them. A potlatch could take several years to prepare and might last as long as 10 days. There could be several hundred guests, and the host was responsible for feeding and housing them all. The potlatch included feasting, singing, and dancing, but the highlight of the event was the giving of gifts. It offered the host the opportunity to display his wealth and

A potlatch house on Whidbey Island in Puget Sound, photographed in 1905.

status. Each person who received a gift became obligated to reciprocate at his own potlatch at some time in the future.

Although the Coast Salish did not have a rigid system of beliefs about gods and lacked a clear concept of a creator, religion did play an important role in everyday life. Special rites were performed in preparation for fishing, hunting, war, or potlatches. The Coast Salish believed that it was important to ask for help from their guardian spirits before embarking on these and other important activities.

Religious beliefs, such as origin myths, varied among the Coast Salish peoples. Various groups, however, did share several fundamental principles. These included a belief in the immortality of certain species of animals.

Because salmon was such a staple in Coast Salish life, many beliefs and ritual practices revolved around these creatures. The Coast Salish believed that salmon were a race of supernatural beings who lived as humans in wonderful houses under the sea. At the time of the annual salmon run, these spirits would dress up as salmon and sacrifice themselves to fishermen for the benefit of humans. After the salmon were dead, their spirits returned to the sea. If fishermen returned their bones to the water, the salmon's spirits resumed their humanlike form, and the whole cycle was repeated the following year. It was essential, however, that all of a salmon's bones be put back in the water; if any were missing, the salmon

spirit might lack an arm or leg, become angry, and refuse to run in the same stream again.

One of the Coast Salish rites that involved these fish was the First Salmon ceremony, which was performed at the time of the first catch from each important stream. This ceremony, which was at times quite elaborate, varied among the villages; however, they all treated the first salmon catch with reverence. The fish was welcomed and honored as if it were a visiting chief; was frequently given offerings, such as eagle down; and was cooked and eaten in a formal fashion. Similar rituals honored other species of fish, such as herring, and both sea and land mammals, such as seals and elk.

Another concept common to many Coast Salish groups was belief in a guardian spirit, which advised and empowered its recipient throughout his or her life. There were two types of guardian spirits: those who brought wealth, rank, or a certain strength and those who gave shamans the ability to cure.

Each person had to go through a quest in order to find a guardian spirit. This was the case even if the spirit was one that an ancestor had previously possessed. After physical and spiritual training, which included fasting and bathing in icy water, a young boy or girl at puberty would search out the guardian spirit, often in remote places. The spirit would eventually appear in a vision. In addition to giving its recipient a certain type of power or skill (such as the strength of a warrior, success in hunting, the ability to weave baskets well, or the ability to cure), each guardian spirit possessed a song with words and a tune of its own. A person would sing his or her "spirit song" at ceremonies, sometimes with friends joining in. Occasionally, a shaman would sing a person's spirit song to help effect a cure.

Usually, spirits traveled around the earth for part of the year, returning to their owners in November during the time of the Winter, or Spirit, Dance. At this time, all those who possessed a spirit would feign sickness. They would then sing their spirit songs and dance for several days until their spirits departed on the next year's journey, leaving them healthy and rejuvenated. During the winter months, considerable time was devoted to ceremonial and religious life.

The Coast Salish constructed both winter and summer houses. Because several families resided in each winter house, the buildings could be 100 to 200 feet in length. The houses were built entirely of wood from the giant trees in the forests. Cedar was most frequently used. Large planks were split, with elk horn wedges, from the trunks of trees and used to create a frame for the rectangular houses. Men then bound hand-split planks, with twisted cedar twigs, to the framework to make the walls. Roofs, which were of the shed type—with a single slope—and floors were also constructed from these planks.

There were no windows, but a hole left in the roof provided ventilation.

Most of the houses contained a centrally located fire pit shared by all of the inhabitants. Platforms, constructed along the walls, served as living quarters for individual immediate families, which included parents and their children. The location of each immediate family was determined by social rank, with the highest ranking situated along the wall farthest from the door. In some houses, each immediate family owned the section it occupied. In others, a chief or wealthy man owned the entire house in which he and his relatives lived. An owner held the exclusive right to carve a representation of his guardian spirit the houses of men and women of the highest rank, some of the interior posts were also carved.

In the summer months, family members migrated from their permanent winter villages to temporary camps on the riverbanks to fish and gather shellfish, and near the mountains to hunt, fish, and gather berries. They constructed various types of summer houses. The Nisqually, for example, built a conical or square structure covered with mats. The Snoqualmie summer house consisted of four forked poles set in the ground with a beam running from corner to corner. These horizontal poles supported a gabled roof. The roof and the sides were covered with woven mats.

Most of the articles the Coast Salish peoples made were for utilitarian rather

THE ORIGIN OF SEALS

American photographer Edward S. Curtis recorded this Clallam myth in the early 1900s. It appeared in a 20-volume collection of Curtis's work, The North American Indian.

"There was a Clallam chief who had a most beautiful daughter, and so proud of his rank was he that he could find no one worthy of her. Hence he was greatly angered when he noticed that she was about to become a mother. But the girl . . . swore that she was a maid. In the course of time a male child was born. Its grandmother wished to keep and rear the infant, but the old chief was too angry . . . and he had a cedar box made and the bottom covered with pitch. In it he placed the infant on its back, and the pitch held it fast. Then he set the chest adrift at the mercy of wind and tide.

"In his novel craft the boy drifted until he grew to manhood. He struggled continually to free himself, and at last, when the hot sun warmed the pitch, he succeeded. Once ashore he set out to find supernatural power, and after a few days he obtained the power of Eagle, and then he came to the home of the Thunderbirds, whose daughter he married. Here he lived happily, every day donning the Thunderbird skin of his wife and thus pursuing whales with the others. His mother-in-law . . . warned the young man not to attempt the capture of the first whale he saw on any expedition, for it would prove to be not really a whale, but an enormous clam whose neck, floating on the water, resembled a whale. This clam was the enemy of the Thunderbirds, and many had tried to catch it .

"One day the young man . . . determined to capture the monster, and he swooped down, buried his talons in the great neck, and struggled to fly aloft. The Thunderbirds from their mountain saw the battle and, perceiving that the clam was nearly conquered, . . . flew down and laid hold of the neck. But the clam only pulled the harder, and almost dragged them all below. Then the young man called upon his guardian spirits, and with a terrific effort the clam was torn from the bottom and carried through the air to the home of the Thunderbirds.

"Now the young man determined to punish his grandfather for the cold-blooded manner in which he had been set adrift. In the form of an eagle he flew over the village, and his grandfather and all the people ran out to shoot at the bird . . . but the eagle was holding the missiles together, end to end, until they reached nearly to the ground. Then swooping down in great circles as if badly hurt, the bird let the line of arrows come within the reach of his assailants. Expecting to pull him down, they laid hold of the arrows, but the eagle flew off over the water and dropped them into the sea, where they became the first seals."

Coast Salish dancer in traditional ceremonial costume, photographed by Edward S. Curtis in 1912.

than decorative purposes. Because they lived in an area of towering forests, it is not surprising that wood was the basic material for much of what they manufactured.

The excellent woodworking skills of the Coast Salish peoples are best seen in the canoes they built. These were made in a variety of sizes and styles. Small, lightweight canoes were used by one or two people for fishing or duck hunting. Tremendous canoes of up to 65 feet in length could carry more than 60 people. These were used for war parties and trips to ceremonies, such as potlatches. A shovel-nosed canoe with blunt ends was made for river travel. Many Coast Salish groups used special paddles that were notched to allow the paddler to brace against roots or boulders along the rivers.

The Coast Salish made all their canoes by first digging out the center of a large cedar log. In order to widen the sides of the canoe, they then filled it with hot water and put it over a fire. When the wood became pliable, the sides were spread apart with thwarts, or wooden braces. Great care was needed in this process so that the sides would not split.

Wood was also used for a number of household items and furnishings, such as cradles, buckets, boxes, and dishes. Boxes were so tightly constructed that they were watertight and could be used for storage or cooking. Oblong, troughlike dishes were also hollowed out of blocks of wood.

The forest provided the Coast Salish with another very important material: cedar bark. The inner bark of the red cedar, or less often the yellow cedar, was torn in long strips from standing trees, rolled into bales, and stored until needed. The bark could then be shredded and softened until it had a cotton-like consistency to serve as swaddling and pillows for infants. Cedar bark could also be split into strips that were weaving material for mats, shirts, rain capes, baskets, or basketry hats. Often, cattail rushes were woven together with cedar to make mats used for mattresses, wall coverings, and fishing boat sails.

The Coast Salish used a variety of different colored natural materials to create beautiful decorative patterns on their baskets and basketry hats: red cedar roots, white bear grass, black horsetail roots, and brown bark from

Three Skokomish women and a child sheltered by a cattail mat-covered summer house in 1912. In front of them is a dugout canoe, the Coast Salish peoples' most common means of transportation between villages.

wild cherry trees. Different groups of the Coast Salish had different styles of basket weaving. There were coiled baskets and loosely twined or tightly twined weavings. Soft baskets were used for storage. Tightly coiled baskets were used for cooking.

Coast Salish blankets and robes were highly prized and often traded to other Indians. Some were made from mountain goat wool or the hair of small,

woolly dogs that the Salish kept. This dog hair was mixed with duck down or the fibers of giant fireweed plants and then spun into yarn.

The animals of the forest provided the people not only with food but also with hides and furs for clothing and with horn and bone for tools. Deerskin was usually tanned and sewn into shirts, leggings, belts, moccasins, and other items of clothing. Hides from

The Coast Salish made woven baskets with a variety of multicolored, ornate, and often symbolic designs. Baskets were commonly used for gathering, cooking, and storing food.

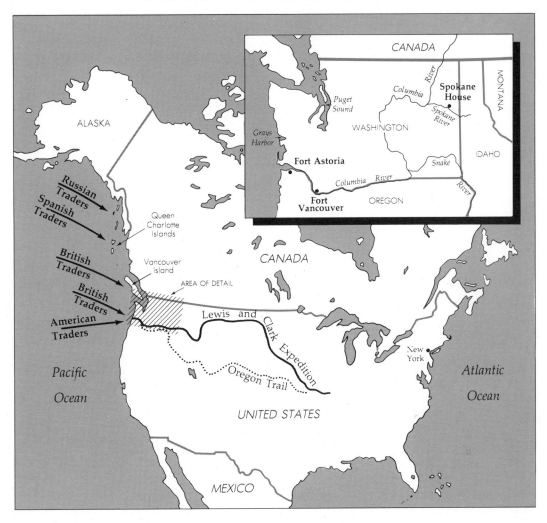

bears, beavers, otters, groundhogs, and other animals were made into winter robes. Elk horns were used as wedges for felling trees and for the handles of digging sticks.

This was the way of life pursued by the Coast Salish peoples when their first contact with non-Indians occurred. Like their forefathers, they strove to live in harmony with nature. But as more non-Indians came among them, their carefully balanced existence would change abruptly.

In 1773, King Charles III of Spain ordered an exploration of the American coast north of Mexico. The Russians had already established a stronghold on the Alaskan coast, actively trading for

An Indian canoe and non-Indian vessel on Puget Sound in 1900. As white explorers and traders began to stake their claims in the northwest in the late 18th century, Coast Salish life changed forever.

furs with the native peoples living there. King Charles was determined to claim the remainder of the coastal land and its valuable resources for Spain.

Juan Perez led the expedition, which reached the Queen Charlotte Islands in 1774. There he met up with the Haida Indians, who were eager to enter into a trade relationship with the Spaniards. Useful and decorative items such as iron tools—which were more durable than those the Indians made of stone, bone, or wood—glass beads, and brightly colored cloth were paid to the Indians in exchange for sea otter pelts. The Spanish traders could get a high

price for these pelts in markets in New York, Europe, and China.

Inspired by the Spaniards' success, the British soon set out to stake their claims in the Northwest. They landed on what is now called Vancouver Island. The native peoples there were equally anxious to barter furs for European goods that were more valuable to them.

In 1792, Captain Robert Gray sailed into what is now known as Grays Harbor at the mouth of the Columbia River. He was the first white American to stake a claim in the Puget Sound area. In 1805, the explorers Meriwether

Lewis and William Clark reached the Columbia River at the end of their expedition. They, too, claimed the area for the United States.

During the early 1800s, the British and Americans were the primary fur traders in the Puget Sound area. In 1810, the British Canadian North West Company set up Spokane House, a trading post near what is now Spokane, Washington. The following year, the American trader John Jacob Astor established Fort Astoria, which was built by non-Indian employees of the Pacific Fur Company on the northwestern border of what is now Oregon.

In 1813, the North West Company took control of Fort Astoria. Then, in 1825, the Hudson's Bay Company, also a British concern, took over Fort Astoria and established Fort Vancouver in the same area. This brought temporary British dominance to the area. But American settlers soon began to head west, following the Oregon Trail to the coast. Their presence helped the American fur trappers already in the area gain control of the Northwest Coast.

When the Coast Salish first came in contact with white traders, relationships between them were, for the most part, peaceful. Trade between the two groups was mutually beneficial, as both acquired goods valuable to them. Iron became a highly prized item in the Indian communities, both on the coast and inland, where it was brought to the

tribes by coastal villagers representing the inland villagers in trade with the Europeans. Many inland tribes, in fact, acquired European trade goods before they even saw a white person. Many never had the chance.

Along with their trade goods, Europeans brought diseases to the Indian population. Coastal Indians—never before exposed to smallpox, measles, and cholera—were quickly infected. Inland villages involved in trade were soon contaminated as well. Entire communities were devastated.

With the westward expansion of the United States and the opening of Washington Territory in 1853 came an invasion of more new people with new ideas for the Indians' land. Speculators seeking quick profits, politicians aspiring to power, and settlers hoping for material gain looked to the land for what it could give them. They saw the forest only as lumber and the deforested land only as farmland. They made salmon, the core of Coast Salish existence, into the basis of a profitable industry. Their demand for furs had decreased the sea otter population to the point of near extinction. When Governor Stevens negotiated his treaties, the Indians of Puget Sound were only a single generation away from those who had first met European fur traders. But in this brief span of time, the way of life of the coastal Indians had been almost completely overturned. ▲

A portrait of Lummi chief Chow-Its-Hoot, who signed the Treaty of Point Elliott in 1855.

2

THE
TREATY ERA

The treaties drawn up by Governor Stevens in the 1850s were intended to place the Indians in Washington Territory on reservations. Nine guidelines shaped his policy toward the Indians in the Puget Sound area. Stevens and his commissioners sought to concentrate the tribes as much as possible; to encourage the Indians to rely on agriculture and other new occupations; to pay the Indians for their land with a yearly distribution of useful commodities instead of cash; to provide teachers, doctors, farmers, blacksmiths, and carpenters for the reservations; to prohibit war and to end slavery among the tribes; to terminate the trading of liquor introduced into the Indian community by white explorers seeking to acquire fur pelts; to allow the Indians to continue to hunt, fish, and gather berries; and, eventually, to allow division of reservation land among Indians.

Stevens believed this was an enlightened policy because it provided the Indians with the resources necessary to adopt non-Indian ways gradually. But he and other officials mistakenly assumed that the federal government would honor the treaties, that the Indians would successfully shift their means of subsistence from hunting, gathering, and fishing to farming, and that all of the tribes could be persuaded that the treaties were in their best interest.

Governor Stevens's treaties established 18 reservations. These were to be administered by three local offices, known as agencies, which were under the jurisdiction of the Bureau of Indian Affairs (BIA) in Washington, D.C. The BIA was established in 1824 as part of the War Department to represent the federal government in dealings with Indians living on U.S. territory. In Wash-

The brash young governor Isaac Ingalls Stevens, who, in the 1850s, convinced Indians throughout Washington Territory to give up most of their land in return for reservations and limited government services.

ington Territory, the Neah Bay Agency would administer policy on four reservations; the Puyallup Consolidated Agency would be responsible for nine; and the Tulalip Agency would oversee five.

Stevens's goals, however, were becoming increasingly difficult to achieve. Congress did not approve the treaties as soon as they were drawn up; therefore their provisions were not to be immediately fulfilled. The federal government also did not attempt to protect Indian land from white settlers. Even before the treaties had been negotiated, the federal government had offered

strong inducements to white settlers to emigrate and settle in the newly acquired Washington Territory. By the late 1850s, they occupied a considerable amount of Indian land. As a result, the Indians firmly believed that they would lose their land entirely.

In 1858, Commissioner of Indian Affairs Charles E. Mix expressed his own concerns with federal Indian policy. He was skeptical about Governor Stevens's original intention in drawing up the treaties with the Indians of the Puget Sound area. The sole purpose of the treaties, Mix believed, was to extinguish Indian title to land needed for the extension of white settlements and to provide homes for the Indians in suitable locations where they could be more easily controlled. It was, he felt, unjust and inhumane to deprive the Indians of their homes and possessions and to relocate them to areas where they could not find their usual means of subsistence. Additionally, it was, according to Mix, difficult to manage so many Indians in an area as large as Washington Territory.

During the early 1860s, federal Indian policy was still inconsistent. Indians had signed treaties but they had not yet received reservation land. Many were beginning to lose faith in white officials. Recognizing the need for a stable Indian policy, the next commissioner of Indian affairs, William P. Dole, urged in 1861 that the treaties be fulfilled. For the first time, goods were distributed to the Duwamish, Suquamish, and Clallam tribes, who had already

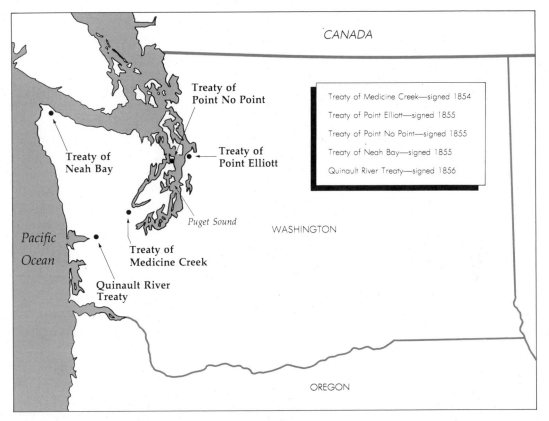

moved onto their reservations. This encouraged the Chehalis, Chinook, and Cowlitz, who had refused to sign treaties in 1855, to indicate their willingness to enter into agreements with the federal government. Besides, the influx of white settlers into the Indians' territory was creating considerable unease in their communities. Dole suggested that a tract of land at the mouth of Black River would be a suitable reservation for the Upper Chehalis and Cowlitz and that the Lower Chehalis and the Chinook could join the Quinault and Quileute on their reservation.

Many other tribes and bands soon requested the reservation land they had been promised; many also requested the opportunity to negotiate treaties. But although the government officials in Washington Territory recommended an increase in the number and size of reservations, the Department of the Interior, which had taken over the management of the BIA from the War Department in 1849, was considering various plans to consolidate the existing reservations. Dole's suggestions for reservation land, therefore, were never carried out.

In fact, Commissioner Dole never really believed that the reservations he suggested should be created. He was merely trying to pacify the Indians who were becoming increasingly anxious about the treaties they had just signed. But Dole shared the position of Commissioner Mix, who had complained in 1858 that the major problem with the management of Indian affairs in Oregon and Washington territories was the difficulty of administering such a vast area and large number of tribes living on widely separated reservations. Commissioner Dole advocated a consolidation of these reservations and remarked in 1861 that it would have been "fortunate if some territory had been reserved in the northwest, as is the case in the southwest, upon which these and all other tribes of that State could be congregated. There is, however, no unorganized territory remaining." This

was a critical point, as many Indians were still awaiting their land.

In 1863, Commissioner Dole suggested that the government replace all existing reservations with two new ones for all of the Indians of Washington Territory. One would accommodate Indians living in the interior, to the east of the Cascade Mountains, and the other would house those on the Pacific Coast. Because the only major natural passageway connecting these two regions is the Columbia River, interior and coastal tribes possessed very different ways of life. Those of the interior subsisted on game, berries, and products of the soil, and were skillful horsemen. Those on the coast were, for the most part, accustomed to fishing and canoeing. According to Dole,

> It is said to be a fact, notorious to all observers, that Indians reared in the interior, and accustomed from

Representatives of the Suquamish tribe staging a protest against the terms of the Treaty of Point Elliott at Olympia, Washington, in 1864.

THE INDIAN TRIBES
OF WASHINGTON STATE

During the 1850s, Governor Isaac Ingalls Stevens presented treaties to the Indian tribes of Washington Territory. In return for their valuable land, the Indians would receive protected reservations and services from the federal government. Some of the tribes signed the treaties; others did not.

Those who rejected Stevens's treaties soon found their land taken over by non-Indian settlers. Those who signed were not all given reservations. Many who were given reservations found the land uninhabitable and moved off it. In time, these Indians with no land to call their own became known as the "landless tribes." Since the 1930s, the landless tribes have been denied official recognition, land, and services from the federal government.

The Landless Tribes in Washington State Today

Chinook ●
Cowlitz
Duwamish
Nuwaha
Samish
Snohomish
Snoqualmie
Steilacoom

The Recognized Tribes in Washington State Today

Chehalis	Muckleshoot	Skokomish
Clallam	Nisqually	Snohomish ▲
Confederated Tribes of the	Nooksack	Spokane
Colville Reservation ■	Puyallup	Squaxin Island
Hoh	Queets	Stillaguamish
Jamestown Clallam	Quileute ●	Suquamish
Kalispel	Quinault	Swinomish
Lummi	Sauk-Suiattle	Yakima
Makah ●	Skagit	

● non-Salish speaking tribe
■ composed of both Salish and non-Salish speaking members
▲ Only part of the Snohomish tribe is currently recognized.

The Treaty of Point Elliott, signed with an X by the Coast Salish chiefs, who did not read or write English.

childhood to its products, cannot be induced to remain upon the coast; and that those raised on the coast, and accustomed to sea-fish and weed, cannot be induced to remain in the interior.

This situation would have necessitated the establishment of two reservations in Washington Territory. They were, however, never created.

In the 1870s, there was a steady stream of white migration to the Northwest. Settlers rapidly began to occupy the more desirable Indian lands, and the Indians were steadily crowded into smaller areas. In an attempt to ease friction between Indians and whites fighting for the land in this area, the Department of the Interior intensified its program of resettlement and con-

solidation. The original treaties had contained provisions anticipating the consolidation, at some future period, of all the bands in the Puget Sound area onto a single reservation. Now, numerous small bands of Indians were being forced onto reservations where they could be controlled by federal officials, and many of the reservations were being reduced in size to provide more land for the white farmers.

In 1876, the new commissioner of Indian affairs, John Q. Smith, recommended consolidating all of the reservations in U.S. territory into just three: Indian Territory in what is now the state of Oklahoma, the White Earth Reservation in northern Minnesota, and the Yakima Reservation in the southern part of Washington Territory. Some Coast Salish peoples were already living on Yakima. Although Smith admitted to having very little information about southern Washington, he singled out the Yakima Reservation as the best place for the relocation of the other Washington groups.

In 1876, Commissioner Smith offered the following reasons for reducing the number of reservations:

Many of the present reserves are almost worthless for agricultural purposes; others are rich in soil, mineral wealth, and timber. Nearly all are too small to subsist the Indians by hunting, and too large for them to occupy in agricultural and civilized pursuits. Many are so remote and difficult of access, that needed supplies can be furnished only at great expense. Nearly all are surrounded by white settlers, more or less numerous. Wherever an Indian reservation has on it good land, or timber, or minerals, the cupidity of the white man is excited, and a constant struggle is inaugurated to dispossess the Indians, in which the avarice and determination of the white man prevails.

Despite Smith's attempt to consolidate the tribes, his plan was never carried out.

The following year, the United States Indian inspector, who was appointed by the BIA to inspect conditions on the reservations, proposed a plan similar to that of Commissioner Dole. He also recommended decreasing the number of reservations in Washington Territory to two, but despite Dole's recognition of the coastal peoples' dependence on their environment, the Indian inspector gave very little consideration to the fish-eating Indians residing along Puget Sound. The

An 1853 painting by J. M. Stanley of Mount Baker and the Cascade Mountains as seen from Whidbey Island in Puget Sound.

inspector felt that the Skokomish and perhaps a few other tribes would prefer to move to a reservation along the coast. Those Indians living on Puget Sound who were beginning to adopt agriculture as their way of life, however, could be consolidated on the Puyallup Reservation. This reservation was centrally located, contained a large amount of arable land, and was now accessible via a branch of the Northern Pacific Railroad that ran through it. Four thousand Indians could be placed on Puyallup, thus vacating 11 smaller reservations in the Puget Sound area.

Despite the various plans submitted by government officials to the Department of the Interior, consolidation of the reservations in Washington Territory never took place. In 1887, Congress passed the General Allotment Act (also known as the Dawes Act), which allowed for the division of tribally owned reservations into small tracts, or allotments, of between 40 and 160 acres. Each Indian on an allotted reservation

Indians canoeing on the lower Columbia River in 1910. This river was the only waterway that connected the homelands of the coastal and inland tribes.

Indians (probably of the Makah tribe) gathering for a potlatch in 1895 on Tatoosh Island, just below the Strait of Juan de Fuca.

was to receive legal title to an allotment, which would then become his or her private property. In an effort to incorporate the Indians into white society, it now became federal policy to treat them not as as tribes or independent nations but as individuals. The Dawes Act granted U.S. citizenship to any Indian born within a U.S. territory who received an allotment or who voluntarily moved into the white community. In 1890, the commissioner of Indian affairs summarized the federal government's

position: "The American Indian is to become the Indian American."

A group in the House of Representatives, however, took a different position on the Dawes Act.

The real aim of this bill is to get at the Indian lands and open them up to settlement. The provisions for the apparent benefit of the Indians are but the pretext to get at [their] lands and to occupy them. . . . If this were done in the name of greed, it would be bad enough; but to do it in the

(continued on page 44)

THE PHOTOGRAPHS OF EDWARD S. CURTIS

One of the most heralded figures in the history of photography is Edward S. Curtis. Born in Wisconsin in 1868, Curtis began his career in Seattle, Washington, where he moved when he was 19. By 1897, he had gained a reputation for his portraits and panoramic views of the scenery of the Pacific Northwest. But in the next year, Curtis found a new subject, the one for which he would become famous—the American Indian. Curtis first photographed the Coast Salish Indians near his home, but he later took pictures of tribes throughout the West.

In his lifetime, Curtis's work was highly praised as a true record of a "vanishing race," as Curtis himself referred to Indians. But most of his photographs were far from accurate depictions of the way his subjects lived in the early 20th century. Many whites at this time had a highly romanticized view of Indians, which Curtis's photographs helped to enforce. He frequently photographed his sitters outdoors, composing his shots so that they appeared less like human beings and more like part of the environment—thus propagating the myth that Indians were at one with nature. Curtis also often dressed his subjects in traditional clothing they no longer wore and sometimes posed them performing traditional activities they no longer did. Ignoring the acculturation and poverty of the people he photographed, Curtis, in the words of an article that appeared in the *Seattle Times* in 1903, "changed the . . . Indian of today into the fancy-free king of a yesterday."

Curtis's works have long been admired as among the most beautiful photographs ever taken. The content of the images, however, say more about Indian stereotypes than they do about Indians themselves.

Two Skokomish women, 1912.

A Salish man fishing with a dip net, 1900.

An Indian navigating the Columbia River in a canoe, 1910.

(continued from page 41)

name of humanity, and under the cloak of an ardent desire to promote the Indian's welfare by making him like ourselves, whether he will or not, is infinitely worse.

Problems with the Dawes Act were apparent from the start. Although the act granted some Indians U.S. citizenship, it could not provide them with state citizenship. In Washington, which had just become a state in 1889, the constitution declared Indians ineligible to vote because, as noncitizens, they did not pay state taxes.

The superintendent of the Tulalip Agency in the early 1900s was highly critical of the Dawes Act. As the person in charge of overseeing many reservations in the Puget Sound area, he observed: "I know of instances where allotments have been made to an Indian without his application, without his knowledge, and without his desire— where in twenty-five years he has never set foot upon his alleged land, does not know where it [is] and does not want it. He is in possession of land that he does not want and citizenship that he does not know, much less understand." Allotment was a completely foreign concept to the Indians. To them, the land was a whole, to be shared by all.

Nevertheless, some Indians readily occupied their allotments and became successful farmers. But they were the exception. The allotments were supposed to contain enough good land to allow a family to make a living by farm-

ing. In reality, little attention was given to the quality of land allotted to Indians or to the interest and ability of their families to farm it.

In his 1895 annual report for the Tulalip Indian Agency, Agent Daniel C. Govan observed that the Indians were not, as a rule, systematic farmers. Some had well-cultivated farms and comfortable houses and were anxious to have their children educated in schools run by non-Indians. But the majority continued to practice traditional subsistence activities. Govan believed that this was extremely detrimental to the Indians. In his annual report to his superiors, he wrote:

A large majority spend most of their time in the canoes fishing, especially during the salmon season. In the summer time they are absent most of the time picking berries. In the early fall, with few exceptions, all, little and big, young and old, go to the hop fields, where they meet old friends from all over the Sound, and east of the Mountains; here they drink, gamble, and, as they say, have a good time generally. This annual pilgrimmage to the hop fields is very demoralizing and positively injurious; but as it has been their custom for many years, and always permitted by former Agents, I did not feel justified in interfering with what they seem to regard as one of their vested rights.

Most of the Indian agents, however, had mixed feelings about this exodus to the hop fields. Life on the reservations

A hop field in the 1880s. Coast Salish Indians could make extra money off the reservations by picking the flowers of hop plants.

was frequently strained by the agents' inability to afford the essential needs of the resident Indians. That their charges could earn money off the reservation by working in the hop fields was a great relief. On the other hand, the possibility of non-Indians trespassing on or taking possession of Indian land that was not occupied during the hop-picking season and the potentially negative influences on the Indians, such as heavy drinking and gambling that took place on the excursions to the hop fields, worried the agents.

Govan, however, believed that the most detrimental influence was to be found on the reservations. This was the older Indian who "still [clung] to his old superstitions and . . . the old traditions and teachings of his savage ancestors." By challenging the new educational and medical practices—brought about on the reservations by Governor Stevens's treaties—and by blatantly expressing his distrust of non-Indians, the traditional village elder was one of the greatest obstacles preventing whites from completely destroying Indian ways. ▲

*A Salish woman overlooking the countryside of British Columbia,
photographed by Edward S. Curtis in 1912.*

MAKING CLAIMS

The adjustment of the Indians of the Puget Sound area to reservation life in the latter part of the 19th century was complicated by several factors: distrust of federal policy, distrust of non-Indians, conservatism of tribal elders, insufficient educational facilities due to a lack of funds and permanent teachers, and poor attendance at the existing schools. Additionally, because most of the reservations were not suited to agriculture, Indians were forced to seek food or employment elsewhere. Many families, while retaining affiliation with their tribes, ultimately purchased land and remained off reservation.

As early as 1870, it had become evident that a considerable number of Indians throughout the Puget Sound area could not, and in many instances would not, live on the reservations. The agent in charge of the Lummi Reservation stated that "the [Samish] and [Nuwaha], two small remnants of tribes, persistently refuse to come and live on the reservation. They would rather live and roam at will in all their ancient and nomadic grandeur." In time, the members of the tribes, bands, and families who rejected reservation life became commonly known as "unattached Indians." Also considered unattached, or "landless," were the various groups of Indians whose ancestors were never given the reservation land that Governor Stevens had promised them or had not signed Stevens's treaties in the 1850s. Many of these groups were now unable to get reservation land.

Landless Indians were scattered from Tacoma, Washington, on the south to Canada on the north and from the Pacific Coast east to the Cascade Mountains. Because of the vast number of their villages, their isolation in many cases, and the local authorities' difficulty in reaching them, the landless Indians received very little attention from the state or federal governments.

At the beginning of the 20th century, federal Indian policy focused primarily on Indians who resided on reservations, an increasing number of whom had assimilated to some extent into white society. But many of the landless Indians also pursued a relationship with the Bureau of Indian Affairs. This consisted of successive unrealized claims for the lands and services Governor Stevens had promised their ancestors. Before 1914, these claims had been individual tribal efforts. The time had now come for the landless tribes to make a unified demand to the federal government.

In 1914, Indians throughout the state of Washington, including the landless groups, joined to create the Northwestern Federation of American Indians in order to pursue their treaty claims. Those Indians who had never signed treaties but had lost their land to white settlers anyway sought compensation for their property. Under the leadership of Thomas G. Bishop, a Clallam Indian, an author, and a political lobbyist in the nation's capital, Indian delegates from the various tribes approved a constitution and bylaws for the new organization on February 23, 1914.

The federation's statement of purpose embraced a wide range of functions: to promote efforts for the advancement of the Indians; to provide means for free discussion on all subjects bearing on Indian welfare; to present a true history and preserve the records of the Indian peoples; to promote U.S. citizenship and all its rights among Indians; and to establish a legal department within the federal government, apart

from the BIA, to investigate and remedy Indian problems.

In succeeding years, the federation would devote most of its attention to the pursuit of Indian claims. According to one member, the federation had been created "for the purpose of digging into [the Indians'] treaty rights which had been neglected and for the purpose of getting the value of the land [taken from the Indians] paid . . . either by allotment or by cash."

On May 20, 1916, Thomas G. Bishop was elected the first president of the Northwestern Federation of American Indians. He submitted to the BIA a large number of Indian applications for enrollment on the list of Quinault tribal members and subsequent allotment on the Quinault Reservation in Washington State. In 1873, the federal government had passed an executive order that enlarged this reservation, which was to be shared by the Quinault, Quileute, Hoh, Queets, and "other tribes of [poor, homeless, or] fish-eating Indians on the Pacific coast."

Bishop represented individuals from more than 40 tribes, including the Chinook, Clallam, Cowlitz, Duwamish, Quinault, Lummi, Muckleshoot, Nisqually, Puyallup, Shoalwater, Squaxin Island, Skokomish, and Swinomish. A significant number of these tribes had already been provided with reservations and allotments, but had been unable to occupy them because they were already being used by other Indians. Some of the tribes, such as the Cowlitz, had been promised reservations, but

(continued on page 57)

SPIRITS IN CEDAR

Before the Coast Salish peoples first came in contact with whites in the late 1700s, the Indians made everything they used from the resources of their environment. Cedar trees, which grew thickly in the forests near their settlements along Puget Sound, were of particular importance. Cedars provided the coastal peoples not only with timbers for building their homes but also with materials for carving beautiful ceremonial and functional objects.

Many of the items the Coast Salish made from wood were used in rituals. At large feasts, known as potlatches, guests were often entertained by dancers wearing ornate masks made of painted cedar. Cedar rattles and wands were carved in the shape of spirits and used by shamans, or curers, to heal their patients. Symbols of spirit helpers also appeared on the painted wooden planks of spirit canoes, with which shamans went on symbolic journeys to search for the lost souls of the ailing.

The Coast Salish adorned utilitarian items, such as weaving tools, with carvings of mythical symbols that they believed would help them perform their daily tasks. These objects were often decorated with images of salmon—the Indians' greatest source of food—to evoke the powerful spirits of these animals.

Since the late 19th century, commercial products have replaced most of their traditional objects. Yet, some Coast Salish Indians still continue to practice the carving arts of their ancestors and pass their skills on to their children.

A carved wooden figure decorated with paint and adorned with two deer hooves. It was probably made in the 19th century by a Quinault shaman as a symbol representing his spirit helper.

49

The pieces of a Duwamish spirit canoe made in the early 20th century. The largest parts (far right and far left) represent mythical monsters who could swallow diseases. Each board's tip is its snout and the painted sun-like figure, its eye.

The dots on this plank represent the songs of spirits. Because spirit canoes were used only once, they were decorated with simple designs that took little time to paint.

Three spirit-canoe pieces, between two and three feet tall. The two smaller ones embody particularly powerful spirit helpers who appeared to people in human form.

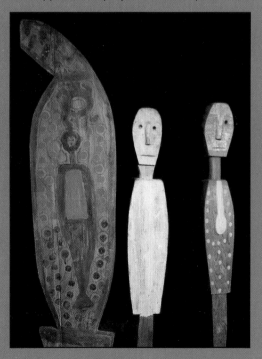

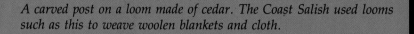
A carved post on a loom made of cedar. The Coast Salish used looms such as this to weave woolen blankets and cloth.

A spindle (the stick) and a whorl (the disk), tools employed by Salish weavers to spin yarn. The northern Coast Salish often made carvings of mythical creatures on their whorls.

Two Coast Salish spindles and whorls carved with abstract designs. A weaver made yarn by attaching goat or dog wool to a whorl and twirling its spindle until the wool was twisted into a narrow strand.

A Cowichan dance rattle made of wood painted and carved to represent a human face. The hair is made of wool.

54

Four wooden wands used by Quinault shamans to cure illness. The three to the right
are carved with images of spirit helpers.

Rattles made of deer hooves strung on
beaded ankle bands, which were worn during ceremonial dances.

*A 20-inch-high mask worn by a Cowichan dancer during the sxwayxway.
This ritual was performed to help individuals who were undergoing great
change, such as adolescents and people who were rising to a higher social
class.*

(continued from page 48)

they had never been created. The enlargement of Quinault provided the federal government with means to accommodate those Indians eligible for reservation land.

According to Bishop, between 2,000 and 3,000 of the applicants belonging to the various tribes in northwestern Washington were eligible to share in the lands and funds of the Indians of the Quinault Reservation. The Department of the Interior disagreed. Eligibility for enrollment and allotment on Quinault would be limited to fish-eating Indians who lived directly on the Pacific Coast between Neah Bay and the Columbia River and met other specific criteria. They had to be descended from those tribes who had been a party to the Quinault River Treaty of 1856; or they had to be members of the tribes for whom the Quinault Reservation was, in 1873, initially enlarged, or they had to be affiliated with the Indians of the Quinault Reservation. Additionally, they could not have received allotments on their own tribes' reservations, and they had to have already taken up residence on the Quinault Reservation. Additionally, each person

A gathering of Snoqualmie Indians in the early 1900s. By this time, many Coast Salish were exhibiting signs of assimilation into non-Indian society.

would have to apply individually for enrollment and allotment on Quinault.

In 1912, the superintendent at the Quinault Reservation had submitted more than 500 applications for enrollment. Many applicants did not provide any evidence in support of their land claim, but according to the superintendent, all "appeared" to be of Indian ancestry. The Quinault tribal council, which governed the tribe and supervised enrollment, passed the applicants as a group without offering any explanation for "adopting" nearly every one.

No attempt had been made to demonstrate that the applicants were poor or homeless or belonged to coastal fish-eating tribes.

Later in the year, the BIA had sent all of the cases back to the superintendent and ordered a thorough review of each. Despite the superintendent's attempt to support the Indians' claims, the BIA still found their applications unsatisfactory.

In 1916, the commissioner of Indian affairs, Cato Sells, requested that BIA special agent Charles Roblin examine

Canoes on the banks of a Neah Bay settlement, 1905. By the late 1800s, it had become clear that many Indians could not or would not live on the reservations.

the applications from 1912 and 1916 and aid each applicant, as far as possible, in supplying the necessary evidence for or against enrollment. In instances when a tribal council had failed to demonstrate that an applicant belonged to the fish-eating tribes, was affiliated with the Indians of the Quinault Reservation in their treaty of 1856, or met any other requirements, a new tribal council would convene in order to supply the information.

Because of the experience of the 1912 applicants, it was obvious in 1916 that many of Thomas Bishop's applicants would not qualify to be included on a tribal roll or to receive land allotments on the Quinault Reservation. Although they were all fish-eaters living on the Pacific Coast, many had already received allotments on their own reservations; and many could not meet the requirement of prior residence on the Quinault Reservation.

The BIA requested that a separate list be made of all applicants who did not qualify for Quinault. This would allow Congress to, if necessary, get a full report about the homeless and unattached Indians living on the Pacific Coast who had not previously received benefits from the government or who had received allotments that were insufficient to sustain them.

Those applicants belonging to tribes for whom reservations had already been provided would have to submit to Special Agent Roblin formal applications with accompanying evidence or testimony supporting their claims. Ad-

ditionally, for the purposes of congressional record keeping, Commissioner Sells required that Roblin get very specific information about each applicant:

> In making the separate [list] suggested, you should so far as possible group families together and show in addition to the names, both English and Indian, the age, sex, family relationship, [percentage of Indian ancestry], and of what tribe or band, where born, and place of residence up to the present time, and if allotted on the public domain or elsewhere; also amount of property owned, and if [applicant has] paid taxes and voted as [a citizen] of [his or her] home [state]. The residence, county and state, of the applicant should also be given.

This information was to be compiled for all landless Indians who had applied for enrollment on Quinault as well as any new applicants who were unattached to reservations and not represented by Bishop. Roblin spent three years preparing a detailed list and report and, in 1919, declared thousands of landless Indians in the Puget Sound area ineligible for allotment on the Quinault Reservation.

The unattached and unallotted Indians of Puget Sound were becoming an increasingly major focus of the BIA's attention at the beginning of the 20th century. They had begun to declare their rights, and Thomas Bishop would continue to represent them as they began to make claims.

In 1921, the Northwestern Federation of American Indians prepared a lengthy document outlining the "Claim of the Indians Embraced Within the Pt. Elliott Treaty." It noted that western Washington was one of the few places in the United States where whites had ever been permitted to settle and occupy Indian lands without the Indians' rights having first been resolved. The report maintained that Indians must now be compensated for the entire tract of land deeded to the United States in the Treaty of Point Elliott. Additionally, it stated that they must be paid the $150,000 that the treaty had promised them and a sum of money equal to the value of the land allotments promised them in 1855.

At the end of 1921, W. F. Dickens, superintendent of the Tulalip Indian Agency, organized another federation meeting. The Indian representatives at this meeting, held in the Tulalip Reservation potlatch house, drafted and approved a resolution offering a summary of their status since the signing of the Point Elliott treaty and an appeal for change:

> [In 1855] homes were promised by Governor Stevens to the Indians. They were promised schools and everything that a kind father would desire his children to have; for nearly sixty-six years such homes promised have been denied, and very few have secured any allotments of lands, and now have no place which they can claim as their home. The Indians of this State have been driven from their original homes and fields which they cultivated, at and before the time the white man came. The best lands have all been taken by the white people, and even the clam beaches and places from which the Indians derived a portion of their living have been taken away from them. The forests have been depleted of game, and the streams of fish, and it is necessary that prompt action be taken in order that the Indians now living may obtain a living, and a position of independence to which they are entitled in the community in which they live.

The tribes had to secure legal representation for the Indians to present their case to the U.S. Court of Claims, the special federal court empowered to hear claims arising from contracts made between the federal government and its citizens. On March 28, 1925, a council was held on the Tulalip Reservation with representatives from the Suiattle, Stillaguamish, and Snoqualmie tribes and from allied bands that did not belong to any particular tribe but had signed the Point Elliott treaty. At this meeting the Indians selected Arthur E. Griffin, a Seattle attorney, and Stewart H. Elliott, a lawyer from Tacoma, to present their claims. Griffin would represent the Indian people under the jurisdiction of the Taholah and Tulalip agencies, and Elliott would represent the Quinault, Nisqually, Lower Chehalis, Upper Chehalis, Squaxin Island, and Skokomish tribes. Few Indians from the Steilacoom tribe attended the

Nursing students at the Tulalip Indian School, 1910. Between the 1880s and the 1920s, the federal government attempted to assimilate young Indians into white society by sending them to boarding schools where they were instructed (in English) in academic subjects and non-Indian trades.

meeting; they felt that their grievances were unique and should be handled as such. Those who did attend, however, soon chose Elliott as their attorney.

The BIA drew up the contracts between the Indians and the two attorneys, and, almost immediately, the advisory board of the Northwestern Federation of American Indians declared them unfair and objectionable. The contracts stated that the attorneys were subject to the direction and supervision of the secretary of the interior and not to the tribe signing the contract;

they gave the commissioner of Indian affairs, rather than the Indians, the right to discharge the attorneys; and they limited the attorneys' term of employment to five years, regardless of the duration of the litigation. Consequently, the tribes made their own legal arrangements with the attorneys.

Arthur E. Griffin became very influential with the landless tribes of the Puget Sound area, more so than Elliott. After he was hired as the attorney for the tribes under the Taholah and Tulalip agencies, Griffin persuaded the

A 1910 photograph of students in front of the Tulalip Indian School. One student from the school later recalled that "[Tulalip] was like a military school. You lined up and marched to almost everything you did."

tribes to reorganize their existing political decision-making processes. Tribal chairmen and councils were elected by each of the landless tribes. Monthly and annual meetings were held to discuss tribal affairs.

One issue brought before these councils was the Indians' previous inability to sue the United States for their claims. The United States cannot be sued without its consent, but on February 12, 1925, Congress had passed a law permitting the native tribes of Puget Sound to sue the federal government for injustices stemming from the trea-

ties of Point Elliott, Point No Point, and Medicine Creek. The landless tribes immediately filed suit.

The Court of Claims, however, did not rule on the case, *Duwamish et al. v. United States*, until 1934, and then the findings offered little satisfaction to the Indians. The Court of Claims maintained that it had no jurisdiction over acts of Congress and would only compensate claims growing out of treaties. For example, the court recognized that the Oregon Donation Act of 1850, which had allowed the confiscation of Indian land in Oregon Territory for white settlement, had cost the Lower Skagit peoples about 15,000 acres. However, the court ruled that they were not entitled to compensation because the land had been taken from them by an act of Congress instead of by treaty.

The Court of Claims recognized the "marked and irrefutable" failure of the federal government to honor the treaties made with the Puget Sound Indians. But it gave them no award. According to the court, those who could prove their claims could not adequately prove the money value of their loss. Furthermore, the 1925 claims law specified that the Court of Claims should deduct the government's counterclaims from the total amount granted the Indians. In sum, treaty annuities paid to reservation Indians, posttreaty moving fees, school administration costs, and health care expenditures accumulated during the 75 years following the treaties amounted to more than $2 million—substantially more than the court voted to repay the Indians. Consequently, the case was settled and the Indians got nothing. Twenty years of hard work had resulted in little more than an education about white people's law. ▲

Chief Shelton and his family on the Tulalip Reservation, 1938.

THE BATTLE
FOR
RECOGNITION

Prior to 1930, an increasing number of Indians in Washington State were beginning to use the courts to battle for their unfulfilled treaty rights. Although they were not always successful, they drew national attention to the plight of reservation and landless Indians. With the election of Franklin D. Roosevelt to the presidency in 1932, a highly motivated and concerned group of men and women was appointed to key positions in the Bureau of Indian Affairs. Led by John Collier, the new commissioner of Indian affairs, they immediately moved to restore the land and acknowledge and protect the treaty rights of American Indians. The major instrument of change was the Indian Reorganization Act (IRA) of 1934.

The IRA marked the end of allotment, which attempted to integrate individual Indians into the non-Indian community, and provided Indian groups with a means to obtain official tribal recognition from the federal government. Those who became recognized could organize tribal governments that could participate in the making of Indian policies. Tribes could also become legal corporations and thereby take over the responsibility of economic development in their communities. The act provided a federal loan system to tribal governments for this purpose. Additionally, the IRA banned the unregulated sale of Indian lands, authorized funds for the purchase of new reservation lands, and directed the secretary of the interior to regulate logging and rangeland grazing in Indian territory.

The IRA applied specifically to "all persons of Indian descent who are members of any recognized tribe now under Federal jurisdiction." It defined a recognized tribe as "any Indian tribe,

Commissioner of Indian Affairs John Collier, 1943. During his illustrious 12-year term, Collier advocated enormous reforms in federal Indian policy.

organized band, pueblo, or the Indians residing on one reservation." Many unrecognized Indians, encouraged by the government's new promise of land and the new qualifications for federal recognition, would now try to change their status.

Recognized and unrecognized Indians throughout the United States began to formalize their tribal organization in an effort to incorporate. Unrecognized tribes also tried to organize in order to secure federal recognition. Simultaneously, the BIA, in its effort to gain information about the country's "lost," or homeless, bands of Indians, began to record the new attempts to gain recognition. It did not, however, recognize them all. Despite efforts to organize, the landless Indians scattered throughout Washington State had the most difficult time receiving acknowledgment and services.

In the late 1930s, the Snoqualmie tried to fulfill the requirements of the IRA. The tribe had never been given a reservation and had never identified itself, to the satisfaction of the BIA, with any of the tribes who had signed the Point Elliott treaty and now had reservations under the administration of the Tulalip Indian Agency. George LaVatta, field agent for the BIA, implied that land was a prerequisite for recognition, and informed the Snoqualmie that it would be necessary to establish a reservation or landholdings for the tribe before organization could take place. LaVatta strongly urged the BIA to provide funds to the Snoqualmie so that they could purchase a sufficient amount of land suitable for agriculture.

In 1937, the BIA recommended that the Snoqualmie purchase, from non-Indian land owners, a tract of land bordered by the Tolt and Snoqualmie rivers. This area, which the tribe could buy with a loan from the BIA, could be designated for all landless Indians of western Washington, who could then be governed by the Snoqualmie. The superintendent at the Tulalip Reservation urged the acquisition of such a reservation.

Unfortunately, a reservation for the Snoqualmie was never created. During the period of U.S. involvement in World War II (1941–45), inflated land prices throughout the Pacific Coast were making land acquisition increasingly difficult. Additionally, the BIA decided that any land it purchased on behalf of Indians had to be able to produce enough revenue to repay the initial cost of the land, or else the tribe had to have enough funds to repay the loan. By 1946, land acquisition for the Snoqualmie was no longer a possibility. The BIA had drastically cut its land-acquisition budget and now restricted land purchases in seven states—including Washington—to areas within the boundaries of existing reservations.

After 1944, the Snoqualmie became less active in tribal affairs. They held fewer annual meetings because traveling had become difficult owing to the wartime rationing of gasoline. At the last meeting in the spring of 1945, the tribe voted to support the war effort and turn its remaining funds into war bonds. Significantly, they also voted to continue to maintain their tribal government and to try to obtain reservation land. Today, the Snoqualmie continue to survive as a tribe, but the BIA has never recognized them or fulfilled its promise to create a separate reservation for them.

During the 1930s, the Steilacoom had also decided to organize under the IRA. Agent LaVatta and Superintendent N. O. Nicholson at the Taholah Agency felt that only about a half of the tribal members met the requirements of the IRA. In particular, many of the Steilacoom had less than one-half Indian ancestry. The tribe then decided to try to join with the Nisqually tribe. This would allow the Steilacoom to move onto the Nisqually Reservation, thereby gaining the recognition necessary to benefit from the IRA, and allowing them to retain their members who had less than one-half Indian ancestry. But Nisqually representatives, recognizing that the Steilacoom had a stronger tribal unity, rejected the idea, indicating their people's fear of the Steilacoom overtaking their community if the two were to merge. The BIA then proposed to transfer the Steilacoom to the Ozette Reservation. But this never took place.

There are no records of further efforts by the Steilacoom to organize until 1941, when attorneys representing the tribe contacted the Taholah Indian Agency in Hoquiam, Washington, and, once again, expressed their clients' interest in satisfying the IRA requirements. Agent LaVatta, at the Taholah Agency, indicated that the benefits of organizing would be somewhat limited due to the war effort but suggested that the tribe might want to establish its identity under the IRA anyway. Nothing more was done.

The IRA completely failed to aid the landless tribes of Washington. In fact, none of the tribes even received the federal recognition necessary to benefit from the act. Those, like the Snoqualmie, who in 1946 were promised federal recognition, a reservation, and services from the BIA were never given them.

In 1947, the Snoqualmie occupied territory in the vicinity of Seattle. They still had not been given a reservation, and few had received homestead allotments on public land. According to the superintendent at the Tulalip Agency, however, the Snoqualmie, who had signed the Treaty of Point Elliott in 1855, had a legitimate claim to land on the Tulalip Reservation. The Tulalip tribes disagreed. Whatever rights the Snoqualmie might have had in the past, they argued, were lost when those tribes living on the Tulalip Reservation were incorporated under the IRA.

In 1950, all of the agencies overseeing the reservations in western Washington joined to form the Western Washington Agency. The new superintendent of the agency, Raymond Bitney, began to question the authority of the Tulalip Tribes, Incorporated. He noted that in the Treaty of Point Elliott the Tulalip Indian Reservation had been "set aside for all of the members of the various tribes that participated in the making of the treaty." Yet those now living on the reservation were claiming the right to manage all of this land themselves. The landless tribes asked Bitney to determine whether their living off the reservation had ex-tinguished their rights to the use of the property.

Dual enrollment (inclusion of individuals on two tribes' membership lists) and confusion in the tribal rolls plagued both recognized and unrecognized tribes. In 1953, the Committee on Interior and Insular Affairs of the U.S. House of Representatives distributed questionnaires about tribal organizations to BIA staff throughout the United States.

When the questionnaires were returned, they included detailed information that enabled Bitney to prepare one of the most accurate and sympathetic accounts ever of the landless tribes. In addition to summarizing the status of the Indians of Puget Sound in 1953, it explained the legal rights of those Indian groups, such as the Snoqualmie, whose ancestors had dealt with Governor Stevens 100 years earlier.

In his report Bitney wrote, "No reservation was created for the Snoqualmie Tribe but they were under the Point Elliott Treaty . . . [The] four reservations created under the treaty . . . were created for the benefit of the signers of the Point Elliott Treaty and not for [the Tulalip Tribes] occupying the reservation." Some of the Snoqualmie lived near the small town of Carnation; others possessed homestead allotments on the unappropriated public domain. A few of the Snoqualmie lived on the Tulalip Reservation, but there, Bitney noted, "we have a situation where there is an intermingling of blood and rights insofar as the tribal properties are concerned." Bitney continued, "practically all of the Snoqualmie people [living on the reservation] are entitled to all of the benefits in regard to service from the Bureau as any of the other Indians and where they have [trust] lands

the Bureau exercises [authority] over the property, the individual Indian money accounts and [the protection of forests]."

Bitney's report noted that the Cowlitz did not have a treaty; in fact, the tribe had refused to enter into a treaty

A 1947 photograph of the entrance to the Tulalip Indian Reservation, administered by the Tulalip Agency until 1950.

IMPORTANT WATERWAYS AND GEOGRAPHICAL LOCATIONS IN WASHINGTON STATE

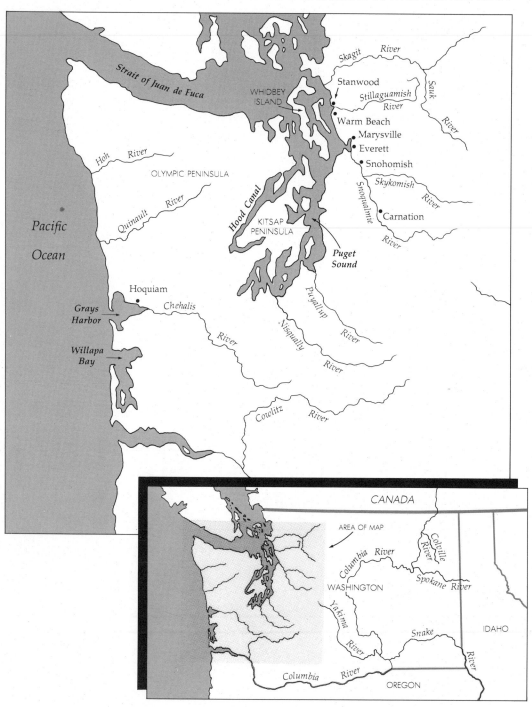

with Governor Stevens and withdrew during the proceedings. The Cowlitz lived, for the most part, in the white community in southern Washington, where many had intermarried with non-Indians. A few of the Cowlitz had received allotments on the Quinault Reservation and, as allottees, would be considered Quinault Indians. The tribe was organized and had hired attorneys to prosecute a land claims suit against the government before the Indian Claims Commission. The ICC was founded in 1946 in order to hear and rule on already existing Indian claims.

The report further stated that the Steilacoom were located near the town of Steilacoom and the city of Olympia and in King County, Washington. During the early 1950s, the Steilacoom tried again to organize. The Steilacoom had no reservation, but they possessed certain rights under the Treaty of Medicine Creek of 1854 to the land reserved on the Nisqually River and the various reservations created under this treaty for the Puyallup, Nisqually, Squaxin Island, and other tribes. They had engaged an attorney to press their treaty claims against the United States and had sued for damages under the Indian Claims Commission Act.

The Snohomish, Bitney explained, originally lived on the south end of Whidbey Island in Puget Sound and on the mainland opposite the mouth of the Snohomish River. After they signed the Point Elliott treaty, a number of the Snohomish received allotments on the Tulalip Reservation and lived north of Everett on Puget Sound, on the Tulalip or Snohomish Reservation. A large number also lived around Marysville and the town of Snohomish and in King County. These peoples were known as the "off-reservation Snohomish."

The Samish had no reservation but claimed to be a party to the Point Elliott treaty. As such, they claimed the same rights as any of the other bands, tribes, or groups that had signed this treaty. The Samish were originally located at Warm Beach immediately north of the Tulalip Reservation and further north near Stanwood. Now they were busy identifying tribal members in order to make their claim to the Indian Claims Commission. The Samish chairman identified 150, "the majority of [which]," according to Bitney, had moved into the white community and "intermingled with the whites and [now contain] a large percentage of white blood."

The report also indicated that the Duwamish had no reservation, although some of them resided on the Lummi, Swinomish, Tulalip, and Suquamish reservations. As the Duwamish shared in the Point Elliott treaty, they were entitled to tribal property or at least part ownership of the tribal property on which many of them lived. In the files at the Western Washington Agency there existed several old tribal rolls listing Duwamish members, but the records had not been updated.

Ironically, Bitney's conclusions were in direct opposition to what the federal government had hoped to learn

A view of La Conner, Washington, and the Skagit River from the Swinomish Reservation, circa 1947.

from the congressional committee's questionnaire. Earlier in 1953, Congress had drafted House Concurrent Resolution 108, which articulated a new federal Indian policy known as *termination*. The resolution stated that "Indian tribes and individual members . . . should be freed from federal supervision and control." The commissioner of Indian affairs had hoped that the questionnaire would help to identify Indian groups in the Northwest that were sufficiently assimilated into mainstream American culture so that the government could officially sever its ties to them, including all treaty obligations.

Bitney, however, cautioned the commissioner against pursuing termination before getting the BIA solicitor's opinion about the rights of the landless tribes. Already the Department of the Interior had developed an administrative policy of nonrecognition for the landless Indians, which allowed it, under the IRA, to deny services to them. Nevertheless, Bitney's report acknowledged their tribal status.

The director of the BIA's western Washington area office, Donald C. Foster, also wrote to the commissioner of Indian affairs in 1953 to express his strong opposition to a single termination bill that would cover all of the Indians of western Washington. Conditions in their communities were so varied and rivalries between some of the tribes so serious that Foster believed a general bill would unleash a storm of protest from the Indians, heir attorneys, and the general public. The tribes in Washington had proved in the past that they would not allow the federal government to ignore its commitments to them without a fight. ▲

Joe Hillaire, a Tulalip Indian, speaking at the Suquamish Reservation in 1963. In 1954, Hillaire helped to establish the Inter-Tribal Council.

5

FIGHTING
TERMINATION

Even before the Bureau of Indian Affairs began to apply the federal government's termination policy to the Indians of Washington, some groups were objecting to its implementation. In the early 1950s, Indians throughout western Washington demanded that the federal government settle the Indians' claims against the United States before terminating its legal responsibility to any of the tribes in the area. They also insisted that the BIA clarify the land ownership status of Indians possessing allotments; that their hunting and fishing rights be protected; and that they be given some tax exemption on their present trust landholdings, for which the federal government held title.

Foster urged the BIA to organize the western Washington tribes for termination on the basis of trust land ownership only. He saw no purpose in the bureau concerning itself with tribes who had no trust property and whose only connection with the federal government was the settlement of their claims. These Indians, Foster argued, maintained tribal connections primarily for the purpose of claims settlement. The BIA should instead concern itself only with the 18 reservations created by Governor Stevens and the allotments given to individual Indians under the Dawes Act of 1887. It should not bother with the 35 or 36 tribes it had previously been dealing with. For the first time, then, the BIA was publicly adopting a policy of no longer concerning itself with the landless tribes because they had no trust land.

It was becoming increasingly obvious that both the BIA and the Western Washington Agency were not being consistent in implementing federal Indian policy. The main issues concerning the tribes in the state of Washington were the entitlement to reservation land and the actual tribal identity of the legitimate successors to those who had signed the treaties with Governor Stevens. During the first half of the 20th century, both recognized and nonrecognized Indians in the Puget Sound area had labored together to secure their treaty rights. As the controversy intensified, a schism would develop between the reservation and landless tribes.

The Northwestern Federation of American Indians, the organization that had been advocating Indian rights in Washington since 1914, disbanded at the end of 1949 with the establishment of the Indian Tribals Council. This organization, consisting of representatives of the various Washington tribes, actively pursued Indian rights until 1954. On February 9, 1954, representatives from 10 western Washington tribes met to organize the Inter-Tribal Council of Western Washington Indians, which would replace the Indian Tribals Council. The Inter-Tribal Council immediately assumed the responsibility for representing the landless tribes. It would continue to do so through the 1960s. Wilfred Steve, from the Tulalip Reservation, and Joe Hillaire, also a Tulalip Indian, tried to get the tribal delegates to accept a constitution and bylaws.

But some of the delegates were reluctant to do so. George Adams, chairman of the Skokomish Tribal Council and dean of the House of Representatives of Washington State, urged the In-

dians to cooperate with the BIA. He stated that the National Congress of American Indians, an organization that represented tribes from around the country, already represented them and that they should rely on this organization rather than create another one. Although Adams was sympathetic to older Indians and their needs, he felt that young Indians should be educated like all other American children and prepared for the changing conditions they would have to face in the future. Adams stated that Indians "should cooperate with the Indian officials to bring about these things as regards education, health, welfare, hospital services and a program for tomorrow and not sit there and talk about the past."

Despite the evident opposition on the part of Adams and some other delegates, a motion to establish the Inter-Tribal Council was made and seconded. The delegates elected Wilfred Steve president and chose a governing body that reflected a cross section of tribes, including the Quinault, Makah, Samish, and Lummi.

The meeting then continued with a discussion of the provision in the Indian Reorganization Act that required an individual to be of at least one-half Indian ancestry to be considered legally an Indian. Martin Sampson, a delegate from the Swinomish tribe, reminded the delegates that the treaties their ancestors had signed in the 1850s said nothing about this qualification; and "the treaty was the only law that the Indians had—they had to hang on to

The 1899 unveiling of a giant Salishan totem pole on Pioneer Square in Seattle (left) and a detail of the pole (right), photographed in 1955.

the treaty . . . regardless of what these tinhorn lawyers say and do about your property, don't betray that treaty, because as long as that treaty is in effect, the Indians can't lose their rights whether they live on or off the reservation." He would soon be proven incorrect.

At the request of the Western Washington Agency, the Inter-Tribal Council presented a report containing objections and recommendations regarding termination policy, which Congress formally endorsed in 1953. Members of the council objected to the proposal for set-

tling inheritances by dividing land among all the living heirs of a deceased allottee. This system resulted in each heir receiving a tract of land so small that it could not be farmed or otherwise used productively. They opposed the revocation of various corporate charters, which would leave some tribal businesses and municipal improvement programs financially unsupported. They recommended that treaty rights such as hospital care be honored and preserved. They also requested that "Swinomish Tribal Community," a legal term describing those living on the

Indian women cooking salmon on a wooden rack on the Swinomish Reservation in the 1940s.

Swinomish Reservation, be inserted with "Tulalip Tribes Inc." in the heading of the termination bill. This would distinguish the Swinomish Tribal Community from the landless Swinomish Indians. Additionally, the report asked that the federal government begin to deal with each of the western Washington tribes individually and not as a single unit. According to the report, "The problems of the Western Washington Indians are not only different from those of other tribes, but because of their original organization in small groups and because of the different treatment by the government are different from each other."

The Inter-Tribal Council met again on February 18, 1954. Lyman Kavanaugh, a Samish Indian, directed atten-

tion to the recognition of landless Indians. He believed that they should be specifically recognized by the council and in the termination bill. Many of the council members agreed. Dessie McDermott, a Snohomish Indian, asked that land ownership not be a qualification for recognition under the termination bill. She also observed that "all non-reservation Indians were treated [by those on the reservations] as poor relations." Termination, however, was never effected in Washington State although Congress did enact termination laws that were applied elsewhere in the country.

Superintendent Bitney began to question the Inter-Tribal Council's authority to represent all of the Indians under the Western Washington Agency's jurisdiction. He cautioned his superiors in the BIA about recognizing the council, which he interpreted as a means to undermine his authority.

For several years, Bitney had been involved in a bitter dispute with Wilfred Steve, president of the council and a former chairman of the Tulalip Tribes Inc. The controversy centered on the ownership of lands and the authority of various tribes to manage these lands. In 1952, Steve had demanded that the old Tulalip Agency site and buildings be turned over to the Tulalip Tribes Inc., because the site had always been tribal property occupied by the Tulalip Indians. Bitney, however, stated that the Treaty of Point Elliott, which had established the Tulalip Reservation, embraced 22 tribes who should have had a share of the property but instead were still disputing the Tulalip's authority to manage it all. Additionally, the agency buildings and school grounds had been purchased by the federal government in May 1860 from non-Indian owners, who had acquired the property under the Donations Land Law of 1850. This law, which had been passed without concern for the Indians' rights to their land, had provided grants of 320 acres to non-Indian American citizens who had resided in Oregon and Washington territories and had farmed the land there for a minimum of 4 years.

Bitney then contacted the attorney general of the United States, claiming that "there is no Tulalip Tribe nor has there been one of record before January 24, 1936." Tulalip Tribes Inc. was created under the IRA in 1934. This legislation was the corporation's only source of authority over the tribal property and rights. But Bitney maintained that its title was invalid because "the true facts were not presented to the Department [of the Interior] when [the land] was turned over to them as there is no Tulalip Tribe." Furthermore, referring to *Duwamish et al. v. United States*, Bitney concluded that because the Tulalip tribe was not recognized, the Tulalip Tribes Inc. could not claim the land.

The Tulalip Tribes Inc. had trouble defending itself against Bitney's accusations. In 1951, the Tulalip Tribes Inc. had petitioned the Indian Claims Commission for a payment of damages be-

The Tulalip Indian School and Agency, 1905. During the 1950s, the Tulalip Tribes, Inc., battled with other Coast Salish groups about who was entitled to income from the use of these buildings.

cause of the United States's failure to act in its interest since the signing of the Treaty of Point Elliott. The Indian Claims Commission had decided that if any of the Indians living on the Tulalip Reservation, or their ancestors, constituted a separate and distinct tribe of Indians, then any territory used by them actually belonged to a number of tribes who had originally been assigned to the reservation. The exclusive possession of that land or territory would not be recognized by other tribes or by the United States. Most significantly, the Indian Claims Commission declared that "it would appear that the Tulalip Tribes Inc. is not a tribe but a community organization." Ironically, the landless and unrecognized tribes had won their Indians Claims Commission cases,

Children on the beach at the Lummi Reservation, 1949.

but they received no remuneration because the federal government made counterclaims exceeding the amount of the award.

In the mid-1950s, Wilfred Steve used the Inter-Tribal Council to further his assault on Bitney. The landless tribes, now betrayed by Steve, refused to support his efforts to remove Bitney from office. Chief Jerry Kanim of the Snoqualmie stated that the tribal council held nothing against Bitney because he was "fair to our Indian[s] and is using our treaty rights on our behalf." As soon as Steve realized that the landless tribes would not support his attempt to oust Bitney, he directed all of his attention to establishing the Tulalip Tribes Inc. as the only legal recipient of land granted to Indians at Point Elliott.

The year 1955 proved to be critical in the landless tribes' fight for their treaty rights. The Snoqualmie tribe objected to the Tulalip Tribes Inc. "running the affairs on the reservation." It adopted a resolution requesting that any income the Tulalip Tribes Inc. received from use of the government buildings located on the old agency site be impounded until the BIA had rendered a decision as to which Indians were entitled to an interest in the unreserved tribal lands not being used on the Tulalip Reservation. The BIA concluded that the title to the unallotted lands on the Tulalip Reservation would belong to the tribes currently living on that reservation.

The fate of the landless tribes of Washington was sealed. The BIA had

Buildings on the Tulalip Reservation along the Puget Sound, 1951. Indians often supplement their income by leasing their waterfront property to non-Indians.

taken a firm stand that the absence of trust landholdings among the landless tribes prevented them from receiving any services and being afforded recognition. This position would be further articulated in a series of decisions made by the BIA when the landless tribes attempted to prepare tribal rolls in the 1960s. One case in particular typifies the bureau's stance.

In 1967, a member of the Snoqualmie tribe applied for enrollment in another tribe in order to receive benefits from the BIA. But as the Snoqualmie did not have a reservation or trust land, her application was delayed. Fred H. Claymore, acting superintendent of the Western Washington Agency, stated: "The Snoqualmie Indians have no reservation and are scattered through Western Washington. The tribe as it existed at the time of the Treaty of Point Elliott *is no longer a recognized tribe* [emphasis added], and the United States government considers the Snoqualmie Indians only as descendants of members of the Tribe as it existed at the time of the Treaty." ▲

A group of Muckleshoot Indians march for their unfulfilled treaty rights, 1966.

6

THE
STRUGGLE
CONTINUES

During the first half of the 20th century, the federal and Washington State supreme courts upheld the Puget Sound Indians' treaty fishing rights, overruling objections from local police and non-Indian fishermen. In 1954, state officials arrested and charged a number of Puyallup Indians for net fishing illegally in the Puyallup River. The state supreme court, however, supported the Indians' right to fish at their "usual and accustomed grounds and stations," as stated in the Treaty of Medicine Creek 100 years earlier. In *State v. Satiakum* (1957), the court maintained that "The Treaty of Medicine Creek . . . is the supreme law of the land and, as such, is binding upon this court . . . and its provisions will continue to be superior to the exercise of the state's police power respecting the regulating of fish."

In the 1960s, the controversy over fishing rights escalated as Washington State officials further attempted to control Indian fishing in the Puyallup River. In November 1963, the Washington State court granted the Washington Department of Fisheries and Game the authority to prohibit net fishing by the Puyallup Indians in off-reservation river fishing sites in south Puget Sound.

Simultaneously, Washington authorities began to harass other Indians fishing off reservation. Their most common tactic was to confiscate the Indians' nets. In order to draw public support for such actions, the Washington Department of Fisheries and Game produced a film that depicted the Indian fishermen as predators who would destroy the state's valuable fishing resource unless they were brought under control.

Indians throughout Washington responded with organized protests. At the end of 1963, the National Indian Youth Council, formed in 1961 by Indian college students, and the newly formed Survival of American Indians Association coordinated "fish-ins" at Frank's Landing on the Nisqually River to draw national attention to the Indians' situation. They notified the media, then openly confronted the local officials by fishing in the river. Non-Indian celebrities such as Marlon Brando and Dick Gregory helped to attract national publicity by participating in these protests.

A number of fish-ins ended in violent confrontation, with state officials using excessive force to stop them. On one occasion, in October 1965, the state launched what the Indians later called a "full-scale anti-riot" operation against a group of Indians trying to symbolically lower a canoe into the water.

Swinomish Indians net fishing, 1938. The Washington State court's 1963 prohibition of net fishing in south Puget Sound led to a storm of protest from local Indians.

Approximately 40 men from the Washington Department of Fisheries and Game, carrying nightsticks and long flashlights (unnecessary in daylight), assaulted this group of men, women, and children. Hal Wolfe, a Republican state senator, described the operation as "Gestapo police-state tactics." Don Matheson, a Puyallup, cautioned his fellow Indians: "This day will be long remembered by Indians. It lets you know exactly where Indians stand in our present society. If you had any illusions about it before, this should serve to dispel them."

Washington State soon began to narrow its interpretation of the tribes' treaty-protected off-reservation fishing rights. In *Department of Game v. Puyallup Tribe* (1967), the state court declared that the Puyallup could no longer have any treaty fishing rights because, according to the court, they were no longer a tribe. The state supreme court, however, did not support this decision. In 1968, it recognized the existence of tribal treaty rights but declared that the state could regulate Indian net fishing on traditional Indian grounds if it proceeded in a nondiscriminatory manner that was "reasonable and necessary" for conservation of the fish.

The Indians' fishing rights still had not been clarified. In 1970, the United States attorney general filed suit in federal court on behalf of the Puyallup, Nisqually, and five other recognized fishing tribes of western Washington, seeking a legal ruling of their right to fish. At the outset of the trial, the pre-

Willy Frank, Jr., a Nisqually Indian and the proprietor of "Frank's Landing," where Indian fishing rights protests, or "fish-ins," occurred in the 1960s.

siding judge, George H. Boldt, invited all groups having any interest in the case to participate as parties. Fourteen more recognized and unrecognized tribes indicated that they would like to intervene.

The case took Judge Boldt three and a half years to decide. The court examined historical records and anthropological information dating back to the signing of the treaties. It reviewed historical analysis of the language—called Chinook jargon—spoken by the Chinook and non-Indian fur traders and later used during the treaty negotiations with Governor Stevens in the 1850s. The court also considered biological data about fish habits and migratory patterns, Indian fishing patterns including the sizes of catches,

Swinomish women with their portion of the day's catch.

Indian trading practices and style of living before and after the signing of the treaties, and the development of state regulations on off-reservation fishing. Judge Boldt's 1974 decision in *United States v. State of Washington* included an opinion on the meaning of the fishing provisions of the treaty rights, the interference by the state of Washington with treaty fishing rights, and the means to reestablish Indian fishing rights.

United States v. State of Washington acknowledged the treaty rights of the federally recognized Indians to fish in their usual and accustomed places. Additionally, Judge Boldt overturned the state regulations that discriminated against Indian fishermen or were not, according to the court, reasonable and essential for conservation. He split the salmon catch among Indian and non-Indian fishermen and established the locations of the tribes' usual and accustomed fishing sites. He permitted the tribes to participate in the regulation of Indian fishing and ordered the state and the tribes to work together to protect and replenish the salmon runs. He also directed the state court to retain legal power to examine the effects of environmental mismanagement on the salmon and steelhead trout resources. To address any specific issues that might arise in regulating the complex fish resources, Judge Boldt also created a fisheries advisory board, composed of tribal and state representatives. The advisory board would hold meetings on fishery management issues and supply the evidence necessary for the court to make any supplementary rulings.

Judge Boldt's decision did not permanently settle the issue of Indian fishing rights as many non-Indians, especially commercial and sports fishermen, ignored the ruling. It did, however, establish the principles and guidelines that, had they been followed, would have resolved the dispute.

United States v. State of Washington was one of the most important cases pertaining to the treaty rights of American Indians in the state of Washington. It was equally significant and controversial in relation to federal recognition of the landless tribes. In August 1974, Judge Boldt ruled that the landless Samish, Snohomish, Steilacoom, Duwamish, and Snoqualmie tribes would be allowed to intervene in the case. These tribes, however, were not only seeking from the court a ruling as to their treaty rights to fish but also a decision on their treaty rights in general and their tribal status. Each of the tribes admitted to the court that it did not reside on a reservation. Each tribe, however, did present evidence to establish that its ancestors had signed a treaty with Governor Isaac Ingalls Stevens and that it was currently composed of descendants of those who had signed.

The Bureau of Indian Affairs, the Tulalip Tribes Inc., and the state of Washington strongly objected to the claims of these intervening landless tribes. They argued that the lack of formal recognition by the federal government deprived these tribes of their treaty rights. George D. Dysart, the assistant regional solicitor for the United States Department of the Interior, repeatedly denied the tribal status of the landless Indians. Deriving his definition from Felix Cohen's *Handbook of Federal Indian Law* (Washington, D.C., Government Printing Office, 1942), Dysart defined a tribe as a "distinct, separate and reasonably cohesive political community or society functioning under a political leadership." He argued that none of the landless tribes met this description.

Lewis A. Bell, attorney for the Tulalip Tribes Inc., stated emphatically that the basic issue when considering

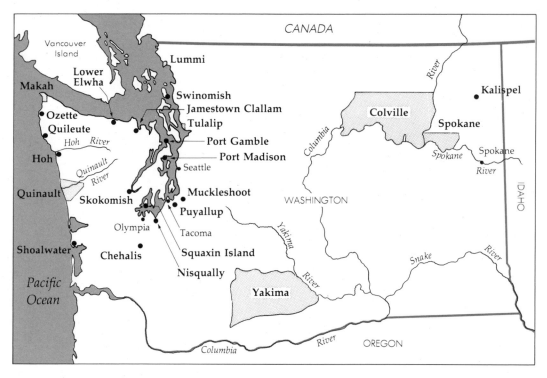

the landless tribes' treaty rights must be whether they had sustained organized tribal structures. He argued that what structure had existed among the landless tribes had not been maintained since 1855; that they had abandoned their tribal affiliation; and that they had only attempted to re-create tribal organization in the 1940s for the purpose of obtaining funds from the Indian Claims Commission.

The attorney representing the Snoqualmie and Duwamish tribes opposed this argument, claiming that the "Tulalip Tribe would have this court believe that the Snoqualmie had not maintained a continuous tribal existence but rather organized and disbanded and re-organized and disbanded whenever it suited them and for purely monetary reasons. This is totally without merit." Additionally, the landless tribes stated that the federal government had recognized their ancestors when they signed the treaties with Governor Stevens in the 1850s and that the government had never withdrawn that recognition or abrogated the treaties. Consequently, the treaty rights were still valid. They also maintained that federal recognition merely allowed a tribe to participate in federal services; it was not essential to the tribe's exercise of treaty rights.

The Tulalip Tribes Inc. further argued that the landless tribes had breached the treaties by not going to reservations and had therefore lost all treaty rights and privileges. But the landless tribes responded that it was unclear whether there was ever a requirement for signers of the various treaties to move to any reservation at a specific time. Additionally, they cited Article IV of the Treaty of Point Elliott, which contained the following provision: "The said tribes and bands agree to remove and settle upon the said first above-mentioned reservation within one year after the ratification of this treaty, or sooner, *if the means are furnished them* [emphasis added]." The tribes maintained that they were never given a reservation to which they could move.

Although Judge Boldt allowed the tribes to intervene in *United States v. State of Washington*, he referred the matter of their tribal status and treaty claims to a master's court, which would render a decision on these issues to be incorporated into the outcome of the case. After a three-day trial in the master's court, Judge Robert Cooper ruled against the landless tribes. Their treaty rights would not be upheld, and they would not receive federal recognition.

The landless tribes appealed to Judge Boldt. He conducted a three-day hearing in which he sustained the position of the United States, Tulalip Tribes Inc., the master's court, and the state of Washington. Judge Boldt held that the landless tribes had not been living as separate, distinct, and cohesive Indian cultural or political com-

munities, nor did the present members of these groups have a common bond of residence or association. Additionally, he maintained that the groups were not descended from any of the tribes that signed the treaties; that the individuals comprising these groups had not maintained an organized tribal structure in a political sense; and that the groups exercised no political authority over their members. Despite several appeals, the decision denying tribal status and treaty rights to the

In 1974, Judge George H. Boldt upheld the recognized Indians' treaty right to fish in their usual places but denied the landless tribes federal recognition and treaty rights.

Samish, Snohomish, Steilacoom, Duwamish, and Snoqualmie was not reversed.

Allen Stay, attorney for the landless tribes, told Judge Boldt in 1974 that when he first read or heard that the United States was going to oppose the intervenors he was surprised: "I couldn't understand why the father would not come out for the son. Then I was saddened. But after I have read the evidence, I am baffled. I can't understand them. I see no point. I am confused. And perhaps this Court is a little bit confused also."

It had been a long and bitterly contested trial. The landless tribes had submitted volumes of records in support of their treaty rights. All major Indian organizations and tribes within the United States who had spoken on the issue of the treaty status of the five intervenor tribes—except the Tulalip Tribes Inc.—supported the claim that all had maintained their tribal organization and recognized them as Indian tribes equal to other Indian tribes. But this was all to no avail.

With the Boldt decision, yet another avenue leading to federal recognition was closed. The 1960s had marked the establishment of nonrecognition as a reason for denying services and treaty rights to the landless tribes. *United States v. State of Washington* had eliminated the judicial means for the landless tribes in Washington to gain recognition. In the absence of such an official procedure, the landless tribes of

Washington State continued to exist in a no-man's-land.

In 1976, however, pressure from nonrecognized groups throughout the United States finally forced the federal government to create an administrative process whereby tribes could achieve federal recognition. The American Indian Policy Review Commission, created by Congress to survey and report on the condition of Indians throughout the United States, had brought to the attention of the general public the social, economic, and political plight of the country's estimated 133 nonrecognized tribes. The stage was now set for a change in federal Indian policy.

The BIA spent a year consulting with tribal representatives, attorneys, anthropologists, historians, federal agencies, state government officials, and congressional staff members in an effort to define procedures for establishing that an American Indian group exists as a tribe. In 1978, the Department of the Interior created the Federal Acknowledgment Project, staffed by BIA members whose job was to determine the tribal status of the nonrecognized tribes. Seven criteria were established that had to be completely satisfied by each tribe that petitioned for federal recognition.

A petitioning tribe had to document its history from first contact with non-Indians until the present, proving that it had maintained "American Indian" or "aboriginal" status; it had to show that a substantial number of its members resided in a community considered American Indian, apart from other communities in the area; and it had to prepare a statement declaring that it had maintained some form of governing body throughout history. A tribe also had to present documentation delineating the tribal laws and the full criteria for tribal membership; it had to present a list containing the genealogy of each tribal member going back to the time of first contact; and it had to demonstrate that the majority of its members were from that tribe and not another North American tribe. Finally, a tribe petitioning for federal recognition could not have been terminated by the federal government.

Each of the landless tribes in the state of Washington began to prepare petitions for the Federal Acknowledgment Project. Two of these tribes, the Samish and the Snohomish, were among the first tribes to complete and submit their petitions. The Federal Acknowledgment Project rejected them both, in 1982 and 1983 respectively.

The criteria that the Samish and Snohomish failed to satisfy are exactly the same as those cited in *United States v. State of Washington*. The Federal Acknowledgment Project staff determined that the Samish tribe had failed to maintain a separate, distinct community; that it was not a tribal community but an organization of people of diverse

Snohomish tribal members discussing their federal acknowledgment petition, 1983.

backgrounds; and that it had no evidence of any tribal leadership or political entity of any kind between 1935 and 1951. Additionally, they declared that the political organization formed by the Samish in the early 1950s functioned primarily to make a claim before the Indian Claims Commission and not in a broader political sense.

The Federal Acknowledgment Project staff rejected the Snohomish petition on the grounds that it came from an organization founded in 1950 only for the purpose of presenting a claim before the Indian Claims Commission. The organization and the ancestors of

A Snoqualmie mother with her child at the Snoqualmie Tribal Office, 1983.

its members did not historically form part of the Snohomish tribe that had signed the Treaty of Point Elliott and occupied the Tulalip Indian Reservation after treaty times. The membership of the Snohomish was composed of the signers' descendants, many of whom had intermarried with white settlers. The Snohomish had never maintained a distinct Indian community, had organized only for Indian Claims Commission purposes, and had no political structure between 1935 and 1950.

The Samish and Snohomish decided to appeal the Federal Acknowledgment Project staff's decision. For nearly 3 years, the 2 tribes were able to extend the 120-day appeal period by filing an extensive request for all of the documents used by the Federal Acknowledgment Project in making its determination. In 1986, however, the Federal Acknowledgment Project staff rendered its final decision. They rejected both the Samish and Snohomish petitions for the identical reasons initially given.

These decisions demonstrate that the Department of the Interior is not likely to back away from the arguments used in the Boldt decision. Other landless tribes seeking federal recognition will probably be faced with the same interpretations of fact in reviews of their petitions. If so, yet another opportunity for them to establish their treaty rights and achieve federal recognition will be lost.

Industrial modernization in the 20th century has brought much change to both the Indian and non-Indian communities in the Northwest. Railroads, lumber mills, commercial fishing, hydroelectric power, and the automobile have altered the area's geography as well as its people's way of living.

As economic prosperity has come to Washington State, many of the Indians living there have lost their most valuable resources. Railroads and highways built, in some cases, without the tribes' permission have overrun reservation lands. Lumber companies have cleared away vast tracts of forest, leaving the land exposed to severe erosion. Hydroelectric dams across the Columbia River and other waterways in the Northwest have flooded many of the Indians' traditional fishing sites. The growth of commercial and sport fishing in the area has also contributed to the depletion of salmon and other fish species so important to Indian life.

In the late 1980s, the federally funded Puyallup Indians took a big step to end this continual exploitation of their land and its resources. In August 1988, the Puyallup voted to drop their claim to some of the most valuable property in Tacoma, Washington. The federal government, Washington State, the city of Tacoma, the port of Tacoma, and private industries have promised the tribe $162 million payable in cash, land, and jobs.

In the 1850s, the Puyallup Indians had signed away millions of acres of valuable land in exchange for a 20,000 acre reservation—which would include the future site of Tacoma. In the 1870s, the Northern Pacific Railroad terminal was built in Tacoma and land on the Puyallup Reservation became extremely valuable. Land speculators began to buy up or illegally occupy much of the reservation. In time, many businesses and industries developed in the heart of Tacoma.

Despite the value of this land, many of the Puyallup Indians are pleased with their deal. Each Puyallup Indian has been promised $20,000 in cash, interest from a $22 million permanent tribal trust fund, a share in 900 acres of tideland and forest in the Tacoma area, and job training. The tribes will also receive more than $10 million in total to build a salmon fishery in the now polluted Puyallup River in order to replenish the salmon runs there. According to Frank Wright, Jr., the tribe's administrative manager, "this settlement will allow us to provide for the destiny of our members . . . [With it], we can protect our culture and our river system. Our people should know they will always have a future."

The future of the nonrecognized and landless tribes does not appear to be so promising. The landless tribes' fight for federal recognition, tribal identity, and treaty rights, which has remained constant through the years, will continue. While many of their Indian neighbors on reservations—such as the Puyallup—are attempting to make a living with their renewed resources, the landless tribes will spend much of their time on the battlegrounds of courtrooms, congressional halls, and countless government offices.

Coast Salish Indians demonstrating for their treaty fishing rights in Seattle, 1981.

Since the late 1970s, however, many have received funds from the Small Tribes Organization of Western Washington (STOWW), which has, for a number of years, been receiving grants from the United States Department of Health and Human Services. With this money, STOWW members have centralized their administrative offices and, when funds have permitted, have hired outreach workers to help tribal members with social and economic problems. Some of the landless tribes have also created community gardens, which

help to feed those members of the tribes who are impoverished. One tribe, the Steilacoom, has opened a secondhand-goods store, the proceeds of which are used to offset the cost of maintaining their tribal office. The tribe has also leased an old building which now houses their tribal museum.

The landless tribes have come to realize that their destiny rests in their own hands. Accordingly, they have developed different types of small businesses, which offer them the opportunity to create jobs for tribal members; to generate funds to operate tribal offices; and to establish cultural centers to educate the public about their tribal history and culture. With all of this, the landless tribes epitomize the spirit of self-determination.

In 1984, the Snoqualmie erected a 10-foot totem pole in the Fall City Cemetery near Seattle. This site had been a sacred burial ground before white settlers arrived in the region. The totem pole would reclaim part of the cemetery as a sacred place. It would also, according to tribal chairman Andy de Los Angeles, inform the local residents that "the Snoqualmie people are still here."

The decoration of the totem pole depicts an important part of the tribe's recent history. Between carvings of an eagle and the Snoqualmie Falls teeming with fish is the carved likeness of Chief Jerry Kanim. Kanim, the last chief of the Snoqualmie, died in 1956. He spent most of his adult life striving to regain the treaty rights of the landless tribes. The tribes will continue the fight. ▲

BIBLIOGRAPHY

American Friends Service Committee. *Uncommon Controversy*. Seattle: University of Washington Press, 1975.

Barnett, Homer G. *The Coast Salish of British Columbia*. Eugene: University of Oregon Press, 1955.

Castile, George Pierre, ed. *The Indians of Puget Sound: The Notebooks of Myron Ealls*. Seattle: University of Washington Press, 1985.

Clark, Ella E. *Indian Legends of the Pacific Northwest*. Berkeley: University of California Press, 1969.

Cohen, Fay G. *Treaties on Trial*. Seattle: University of Washington Press, 1986.

Elmendorf, W. W. *The Structure of Twana Culture*. Pullman: Washington State University Press, 1960.

Horr, David Agee, ed. and comp. *Coast Salish and Western Washington Indians II*. New York: Garland, 1974.

Ruby, Robert H., and John A. Brown. *A Guide to the Indian Tribes of the Pacific Northwest*. Norman: University of Oklahoma Press, 1986.

———. *Indians of the Pacific Northwest*. Norman: University of Oklahoma Press, 1981.

Smith, Marian W. *The Puyallup-Nisqually*. New York: Columbia University Press, 1940.

Suttes, Wayne. *Coast Salish Essays*. Seattle: University of Washington Press, 1988.

THE COAST SALISH PEOPLES AT A GLANCE

There are approximately 30 major Salish-speaking Indian groups living in Washington State today. Some 20 of these groups are currently recognized by the U.S. government, but there are many Indian peoples who have lost their tribal status and are now involved in legal action to regain recognition.

CULTURE AREA *Northwest Coast*

GEOGRAPHY *Puget Sound area of Washington State*

LINGUISTIC FAMILY *Coast Salish*

CURRENT POPULATION *Approximately 25,000 recognized; approximately 4,500 unrecognized*

FIRST CONTACT *Unknown but most likely British and American fur traders in the 18th century*

FEDERAL STATUS *Approximately 20 recognized and at least 10 unrecognized Salish-speaking tribes in Washington State*

GLOSSARY

agent A person appointed by the Bureau of Indian Affairs to supervise U.S. government programs on a reservation and/or in a specific region. After 1900 the title *superintendent* replaced *agent*.

allotment U.S. policy applied nationwide through the General Allotment Act of 1887 that aimed to break up tribally owned reservations by assigning individual farms and ranches to Indians. Allotment was intended as much to discourage traditional communal activities as to encourage private farming and assimilate Indians into mainstream American life.

anthropology The study of the physical, social, and historical characteristics of human beings.

Bureau of Indian Affairs (BIA) A U.S. government agency now within the Department of the Interior. Originally intended to manage trade and other relations with Indians, the BIA now seeks to develop and implement programs that encourage Indians to manage their own affairs and to improve their educational opportunities and general social and economic well-being.

culture The learned behavior of humans; nonbiological, socially taught activities; the way of life of a group of people.

Department of the Interior U.S. government office created in 1849 to oversee the internal affairs of the United States, including government land sales, land-related legal disputes, and American Indian issues.

dialect A regional variant of a particular language with unique elements of grammar, pronunciation, and vocabulary.

dowry The money and/or property presented to the family of a future husband by the family of his future wife.

guardian spirit quest A fast and vigil undertaken by Indian youths in the hope of receiving a sign from a supernatural power who might guide and protect them throughout their life. The vigil usually required a person to stay outdoors alone for an extended period of time.

hop fields The places in which hop plants are grown. The dried flowers of the plant are collected to obtain an oil used in brewing beer. The Coast Salish made annual pilgrimages to these fields to meet with family and friends.

Indian Claims Commission (ICC) A U.S. government body created by an act of Congress in 1946 to hear and rule on claims brought by Indians against the United States. These claims stem from unfulfilled treaty terms, such as nonpayment for lands sold by the Indians.

Indian Reorganization Act (IRA) The 1934 federal law that ended the policy of allotting plots of land to individuals and encouraged the development of reservation communities. The act also provided for the creation of autonomous tribal governments.

Oregon Trail Route used by non-Indian settlers who moved to the Pacific Northwest coast from the central and eastern portions of the country from the 1840s through the 1860s. The trail crossed the traditional homelands of many of the Coast Salish peoples.

potlatch A special feast, held by many societies in the Pacific Northwest, during which the host gave gifts and food to many guests in order to establish or increase his status. A smaller potlatch might also be held to inaugurate a new house, commemorate the death of a village member, or celebrate a marriage or the naming of a chief's heir.

reservation, reserve A tract of land retained by Indians for their own occupation and use. *Reservation* is used to describe such lands in the United States; *reserve*, in Canada.

spirit canoe A construction made of painted wooden planks that were placed upright into the ground in the shape of a canoe. The Coast Salish used a spirit canoe in a curing ceremony during which the participants pantomimed an expedition to search for a tribe member's lost soul.

termination Federal policy to remove Indian tribes from government supervision and Indian lands from trust status; in effect from the late 1940s through the 1960s.

territory A defined region of the United States that is not, but may become, a state. The officials of a territory are appointed by the president, but territory residents elect their own legislature.

totem The emblem or symbol of a clan or family, usually an animal or plant that the family claims as its mythical ancestor. These images were carved into Coast Salish totem poles and house posts.

treaty A contract negotiated between representatives of the U.S. government or another national government and one or more Indian tribes. Treaties may deal with the cessation of military action, the surrender of political independence, the establishment of boundaries, terms of land sales, and/or related matters.

tribe A social unit consisting of several or many separate communities united by kinship, culture, and language, and such other social institutions as clans, religious and economic organizations, and warrior societies.

trust The legal term dating from the late 19th century for the relationship between the federal government and many Indian tribes. Government agents managed Indians' business dealings, including land transactions and rights to natural resources, because the Indians were considered legally incompetent to manage their own affairs.

unattached Indians The name first used in the 1870s to describe members of Coast Salish groups who were left landless because their ancestors had refused to move onto reservations, had never received such lands, or could not sustain themselves on the lands they were given.

weir A wooden fence constructed in a stream to trap fish or force them into a narrow channel where they can easily be netted.

PICTURE CREDITS

FRANK W. PORTER III is general editor of INDIANS OF NORTH AMERICA and director of the Chelsea House Foundation for American Indian Studies. He earned his B.A., M.A., and Ph.D. from the University of Maryland and is the author of *The Nanticoke* (1988), also in this series, as well as of *In Pursuit of the Past: An Anthropological and Bibliographic Guide to Maryland and Delaware* (1986) and *Native American Basketry: An Annotated Bibliography* (1988). Dr. Porter is currently working with several of the Coast Salish peoples of the Pacific Northwest in their efforts to gain federal status as recognized tribes.